Way Beyond The Blue

Dylan Morrison

Way Beyond The Blue
ISBN-13: 978-1495908682
ISBN-10: 1495908682

Copyright © 2014 Dylan Morrison

The right of Dylan Morrison to be identified as the author of this work has been asserted in accordance with sections 77 and 78 of the Copyright, Designs and Patents Act 1988.

The cover image is the copyright of David Hayward, 2014. All rights are reserved.
The cover design is the copyright of Ping Creative Ltd 2014. All rights are reserved.
Way Beyond The Blue Is published by Dylan Morrison Publishing.

To those whom I've met along the Way; especially my Soul Mate, Zan. Without her love, patience and understanding I'd have fallen into a deep, dark ditch many moons ago.

Contents

Acknowledgments

Prologue

Part 1: *Mystics And Their Sayings*

1	Augustine Of Hippo (354-430 AD)	1
2	The Unknown Author Of 'The Cloud Of Unknowing' (14th Century)	4
3	William Law (1686-1761)	6
4	George MacDonald (1824-1905)	9
5	Hugh of St. Victor (1078-1141)	12
6	Ruysbroeck (1293-1381)	15
7	The unknown author of 'The Cloud Of Unknowing' (14th Century)	17
8	Fenelon (1651-1715)	21
9	14Francis De Sales (1567-1622)	25
10	John Martin Sahajananda (born 1955)	30
11	Madame Guyon (1648-1717)	35
12	Gerhard Tersteegen (1697-1756)	39

Part 2: *Mystical Musings*

13	Hot Or Cold Spirituality?	47
14	Rivers & Buckets ~ Part 1	50

15	Rivers & Buckets ~ Part 2	54
16	Spiritual Ecosystems	58
17	Inner Peace	63
18	Eden's Desire	68
19	Go Man Go	74
20	Mimetic Desire & Human Lids	80
21	What's So Special About Yeshua?	83
22	Why Do I Feel Weird In Church?	91
23	Dysfunctional Religious Attachments	95
24	Inner Space 1 ~ To Boldly Go Where No Preacher's Gone Before	100
25	Inner Space 2 ~ The Egg & Our Inner World	105
26	Inner Space 3 ~ Sacred Unity	109
27	Inner Space 4 ~ Fake Faith	114
28	Inner Space 5 ~ The Road To Wholeness	120
29	Yeshua Sayings That You Rarely Hear In Church ~ 1	125
30	Yeshua Sayings That You Rarely Hear In Church ~ 2	130
31	Yeshua Sayings That You Rarely Hear In Church ~ 3	135
32	Yeshua Sayings That You Rarely Hear In Church ~ 4	141

33	The Inner Void	146
34	Friends	150
35	Anam Cara ~ Soul Friend: Part 1	154
36	Anam Cara ~ Soul Friend: Part 2	157
37	Two-Way Traffic: Part 1	161
38	Two-Way Traffic: Part 2	165
39	Two-Way Traffic: Part 3	170
40	Will I Or Won't I? ~ Part 1	173
41	Will I Or Won't I ~ Part 2	177
42	Will I or Won't I? ~ Part 3	181

Epilogue

Glossary of Important Terms

About The Author

Acknowledgements

There have been many fellow travellers who've helped bring this, my second publication, to fruition. Zan, my wife of over thirty three years, continues to be an inspiration to me, as she presses on in her own determined journey of self-discovery. On a practical level, her many hours of dog sitting and tea making have enabled me to retreat to my study, where this published material first saw the light of day. Thanks Zan for being you, the patient one in our ever changing life together. I've led you up many religious dead ends in my search for the Divine. Your decision to stay by my side throughout it all has given me the clearest glimpse of the Love that we both seek.

I wish to thank all those *new* friends that I've met on social media sites over the last few years, for their interest in what I have to say. While not always agreeing with my mystical take on things, their rich collage of spiritual and religious backgrounds has inspired me to think further out of the Yeshua box than I would have previously dared. Our common desire to find the Love behind it all, has wonderfully joined us in one spirit.

David Hayward, the wonderful Canadian artist responsible for the front cover of this edition, has captured the essential spirit of my continuing journey. My little, black dog and *healer,* Suki, is also thrilled that David has placed her beside me in this beautiful piece, *Walk At Dusk.*

At such times, the Divine has often drawn close to us in isolated rural Lincolnshire. May I encourage you to view David's prophetic art work online. You will be surprised at how often he hits the nail of religious hypocrisy on the head. Thank you, David, for graciously allowing your work to grace the cover of *Way Beyond The Blue*.

I would, yet again, like to acknowledge the role of Spirit, the Divine Breath, in my writing, especially that contained within *Way Beyond The Blue*. It may sound presumptuous, certainly clichéd to credit the Divine with my literary efforts and yet as I sit down to write, the thoughts are dictated to me from somewhere deep within. I believe this source to be spirit spark, that sense of *Other,* that visitor from the fields of Transcendence. In Yeshua's language, Holy Breath. Thank You for the shared intimacy of your inspiration.

Finally, my dear readers, thank *you* for exploring my little literary offering to Love. I believe that, beyond space-time, all shall gather, Way Beyond The Blue, when words will cease and Love will have its Way.

Dylan Morrison
Lincoln, England
March 2014

Prologue

The world system, both political and economic, has, yet again, descended into a state of confused chaos, like some old, creaky, runaway steam-train about to veer off its highly dysfunctional tracks. The common man, stunned by the financial crash of 2007-2008, remains disillusioned with the leadership of all political cowboys, equipped with their six-shooters, honed egos, and unreformed, highly inflated expense accounts. The answer doesn't seem to lie there then!

Dictators have discovered, much to their surprise, that their people don't love them after all, falling like nine pins after years of totalitarian repression, only to be replaced by an alternative, but often more brutal, despotic clone or system. World economies tentatively creep out from under their huge debts, tentatively promising better times ahead, yet nobody is really convinced. As the merchant bankers run back into their financial rabbit holes of denial to declare 'Business As Usual!' the working poor give out a collective groan.

With our rat-race, oil-obsessed society in such a confused state of flux, does the religio-spiritual world have the much sought-after answers? Apparently not. Ineffective and largely irrelevant, institutional religion either hides behind its whitewashed church walls, issuing meaningless platitudes or turns to the hip *business model,* serving frothy cappuccinos to desperate seekers while adorning their purpose-built foyers with portrait sized photos of their *awesome* chief executives; the latter being the 21st century incarnations of the professional pastor, reverend, priest – now with professionally-whitened teeth and casual Armani outfits to match.

Is it any wonder that the angst-ridden spiritual seeker is turning more and more to Western, Mind, Body, Spirit gurus, the beatific cloned offspring of their devout Eastern Masters? What have these guys and gals got that our old time religion has missed out on? In my humble opinion, the answer is quite simple viz. *Mystery* and its derivative *Mysticism*.

Since my first encounter with *Other* or *Spirit* at the tender age of five, I've been on a roller coaster journey to try and tie down this shadowing Presence that draws alongside mankind in his brokenness. Staring with a child's eyes at the cloudless heavens of those balmy summer days of the 1960s, I somehow sensed that my new friend, Other, was out there somewhere, *way beyond the blue*.

Following my teenage conversion to Evangelical Christianity, I thought I'd found the answer in the portrait of Jesus Christ, as painted by my kind-hearted but, nevertheless, zealous mentors. So convinced was I by their spiritual paradigm, that years later I abandoned my Mathematics teaching post to work for a radical Christian sect in my homeland of Northern Ireland. However, the trouble was, that, like a new pair of tight, trendy trousers, it only fitted for a while before being torn asunder by the intervention of reality viz. the loss of my son, Ben.

Yet, in those heady days of prayer, praise and evangelism, I first came in contact with the spiritual teachings of the largely unknown, Christian mystics. Their pietistic writings, wafting a tangible sense of the Divine Presence made me thirst for more; for that communion with Spirit, which, they claimed, was the purpose of my existence.

It shouldn't have come as a great surprise then, that sixteen years after chucking in dogma based religion, my return to spiritual faith came about through two separate, but strangely similar, mystical experiences, as recounted in my first book, *The Prodigal Prophet*. I was back on the mystical path, following the greatest of all mystics, Yeshua bar Yosef, the Jewish Nazarene. It is to Him and the Divine Spirit-Breath that I owe my new life – a life of mystery, but also one of comforting Presence and sound purpose. I believe this unusual way of life to be the treasured pearl of great price that Yeshua still offers to our broken society of the 21st century.

May I point out to my readers that, although I commonly refer to God or Divine Love as *He* in my writing, I believe the Ultimate Source of All to be beyond gender labels whether male, female or indeed neither. Patriarchal, Divine Feminine and non-personal Energy attempts to describe Divine Love are just that, attempts. All have something valuable to contribute towards our understanding of the Divine workings yet none can fully grasp the One who is Mystery, the Creator of all space-time genders. For the sake of simplicity I have stuck with the commonly accepted personal pronoun that I was raised with back in the Bible Belt of Northern Ireland. I trust that my more progressive readers will understand my decision and not read too much into it.

The following work is split into two main sections:

In *Part 1*, I consider a collection of profound sayings from past and present mystics, examining their relevance for today.

In *Part 2*, I've tapped into my own personal stream of consciousness. Hopefully, images, insights and practical wisdom will flow from each page, helping you, the reader, to step out of limiting, concept-focused religion and into the place of Mystery. May I humbly suggest that it is here, in this prototypal Holy of Holies, where we'll encounter the naked, simple profundity of Divine Presence and its Unconditional Love.

Dylan Morrison

Part One

Mystics And Their Sayings

1

Augustine Of Hippo (354-430 AD)

"O God, You have made us for Yourself, and our hearts are restless till they rest in You."

According to his autobiographical *Confessions*, Augustine was quite a lad in his youth. Wine, women and song seemed to be the hedonistic path his early life followed. His sudden conversion in the beauty of a garden took him completely by surprise.

One of the greatest theologians of the early church, Augustine became the bishop of Hippo Regius in Roman North Africa. I've some major problems with Augustinian theology as he introduced the ingenious, yet diabolical, concept of original sin into Western Christianity. As a result of my own religious journey I believe this Augustinian doctrine to have an extremely negative influence on our view, both of man and of God, but that's a story for another day.

I tend to think that Augustine was perhaps, a bit preoccupied with paralysing guilt for the so called 'sins of the flesh' that plagued his youthful endeavours.

Unfortunately his unbalanced view of human sexuality still blights both men and women in the religious world.

However, the good news is that, despite such a dismal view of man's nature, Augustine came up with the wonderfully profound saying above. Here are just a few, question and answer based thoughts on his words:

Why are we here?

We've been created by the Divine for Himself. What a humbling answer.

Did He do it to make a lot of little puppets or religious slaves?

Definitely not. He wanted an extended family to share His being, one that He could pour out His unconditional love upon.

We humans are a pretty restless bunch. Why?

Our restlessness is the result of our inner desire for wholeness or happiness. We'll try anyone or anything to satisfy this existential craving but nothing works for very long. Our frustrated desire ultimately births violence between individuals, families and indeed nations. All violence is the love child of desire, the desire for Being, the desire for Belonging. Addictions and their accompanying behaviours lie at the extreme end of the search for wholeness spectrum. Anything has the potential to prove addictive - even religion and, dare I say it, even Christianity.

What cures this continual restlessness?

A spiritual encounter with the Divine. Not a religious belief system but a breakthrough by the transcendent Other into our psychic wiring. This awakening, enlightenment or conversion is the key to our restlessness problem. To drink of Divine Presence like a suckling babe at the mother's breast, is the place of peace, the place of rest and homecoming. All the great mystics within the Christian tradition saw this encounter as the key to solving the inherent angst of the human condition.

Finally, a slightly disturbing yet important question to mull over.

How much does our religious enthusiasm and activity stem from a spiritual restlessness?

From my own experience I'd have to say quite a lot. Perhaps this is the main reason why so many once enthusiastic adherents drop out of organised religion. Ultimately, religious belief and external practices are powerless to still our storm of restlessness. Disillusionment will drive the ex-devotee to try for their fix elsewhere.

Dylan Morrison

2

The Unknown Author Of 'The Cloud Of Unknowing' (14th Century)

"By love He may be grasped and held; but by thought never."

What a radical thought from this unknown author who probably was a highly regarded scholar and monk. He strongly suggested that only those dedicated to living the Christ life should read his writings; that they aren't for the eyes of atheists nor agnostics. I'm not sure I agree.

Just consider how many theological and philosophical treatises have been written about the Divine since time immemorial. Does the study of these often ingenious works bring one into a direct encounter or awareness of such a Presence?

I think not.

Theologically based religion is not the way to know God. In fact, I believe that it often drives Divine Presence away, like a sensitive butterfly leaving a fragrant flower due to excessive examination by a close observer. Analysis and classification are certainly useful tools for scientific measurement and enquiry but not for a God search. By definition, the essence of God, the Origin of all, must lie beyond words and concepts. If it wasn't then He wouldn't be God. This apparent barrier in our consciousness is *The Cloud of Unknowing* that our medieval author is referring to.

How then can we expect to *meet* God, if He is so transcendent?

Only by a sometimes feeble, yet growing love can we make contact with our Source, Sacred Unity. Such love, often birthed in our human brokenness is the laser-like means by which we break through the limits of reason. However, the really good news is that initially the Divine makes contact with us through an experience of His unconditional Love. Hence there exists a profound two-way traffic in the transfer of love between God and man.

Theological theories are well and good, if you like a good discussion. However, in my own experience, whilst promising much, they just lead down a dark, dead-end, tunnel where I still hunger for the Divine touch. Perhaps stillness and contemplation reap more lasting, inner-dividends than the multitude of sermons and theories that we're bombarded with by verbose religious experts.

3

William Law (1686-1761)

"The sun doesn't meet the springing bud that stretches towards him with half the certainty that God, the source of all good, communicates Himself to the soul that longs to partake of Him."

William Law was a friend and associate of John Wesley's until they fell out over Law's later views on Christian mysticism. Why are such fractures in relationships commonplace within the religious community? The answer, I believe, is quite simple. In religious thought, dogma is often ranked above the wholeness or holiness of unity, surely the true aim of all spiritual life. Anyway, let's get back to this little gem of a saying.

As I write, springtime has just come upon us here in rural Lincolnshire, England. It's certainly the right time of year to be contemplating sunshine and buds. I'm so amazed that buds don't have to work hard at growing, eventually turning into flowers or blossom without any great effort.

The buds amazing growth secret appears to lie within their DNA. They just sit there pointing towards the sun. Neither do they choose their position on the plant or tree; they were just destined to be there. In reality, it's the far flung sun that does all the hard work of growth, generating the heat and light required to make the bulbs reach their full potential.

Does my allegorical line of thought sound like the oft frowned upon, practice of passive Quietism?

Perhaps it does. In light of past experiences, I now believe that we're only asked to point ourselves in the direction of God, with total honesty, even if we find ourselves broken and lying in the psychological gutter. Divine Presence will come as surely as the sun shines on the bud in its aloneness.

The phenomenon of desire has been hardwired into us neither for the accumulation of relational nor material attachments but as a gift that leads us toward the Divine. The only connection that ultimately satisfies the human ache for meaning is the embrace by ultimate reality.

Existentialists aren't sure there is anything or anyone to be embraced by, yet take the leap of faith anyway. On the other hand many religious folk are just glad to be a bud, stopping short of an intimate experience of the flow of Divine energy that surrounds them.

Who is the Divine willing to bathe in His rays of enlightenment?

The answer is truly good news; not only religious believers, but all mankind. Yeshua has turned the whole God equation upside down - there is no *them and us*, no *in or out* as far as the Divine is concerned. Such dualistic categories are products of the religions that foolishly try to monopolize Him.

At least that's my penny's worth, born out of a painful faith journey through the minefield of dualistic Irish religion.

Why do we make it all so complicated?

4

George MacDonald (1824-1905)

"He shall have purity."

The renowned English author, C S Lewis, was a fan of George MacDonald's religious thought, inspiring him to produce an anthology of the best of MacDonald's sayings. MacDonald himself was a minister in the Calvinistic Church of Scotland, who focused so much on the Love of God that it got him into deep water with his critical congregation. They even tried to get rid of poor George by annually reducing his salary. However, heading into poverty, MacDonald kept preaching that no-one would be eternally punished by God. He refuted the Calvinistic view of the afterlife as a contradiction of Divine Love.

At first glance, the above saying sounds extremely simple but is, on further examination, stunningly profound. Most religious observers view it through the traditional spectacles of morality. In other words, the purity referred to is usually interpreted as moral or ethical purity, the keeping of some tantalisingly unobtainable Divine gold standard. God's determination to achieve such purity sounds like the prosecution's plea for Divine vengeance.

I am of the opinion that such an interpretation is skewed and deeply flawed. In His essence, God is Divine Love; yes, an all-consuming fire, but a fire of Love. Purity, at its linguistic root, denotes *singleness, without mixture, of one substance.* Yeshua claimed that the pure in heart would see God. Did he mean that the morally perfect would view the Divine? I believe not.

A better rendering of the Nazarene's original Aramaic words declare, *'the single or non-fragmented heart shall see God'.* Our Western world view is a truly fragmented one. Socially, politically and even religiously we're split into *them and us.* Scientific rationalism and inquiry have classified the Cosmos into little separate boxes in order to aid methodical analysis. I believe that such a fragmented view eventually leads to deep suffering within the delicate human psyche.

The answer to this often hidden angst within the human heart, is to observe the unity of all things and to leave behind the dualistic specs through which we view our lives. If, as quantum theory suggests, we are, at our irreducible minimum, just a bunch of conscious energy, then we're already one with the energy field of creation and indeed the Divine Father Himself. Our apparent separateness is, in reality, a psychological illusion that leads to violence and a permanent state of restlessness.

Seen in this light MacDonald's statement is now good news. Instead of delivering a divine threat, the saying now encourages us that God is a God of unity, the one source from whom all creation flows. We're already unified, at one with each other and indeed the Divine Himself. No spiritual or religious gymnastics are required to get us there; it's already a higher reality from which we can, even now, draw the benefits. Is it not time to re-interpret Yeshua's words without our dualistic lenses?

Dylan Morrison

5

Hugh of St. Victor (1078-1141)

"His love is single, but not private; alone, yet not solitary; shared but not divided; growing no less by sharing, failing not through use, nor growing old by time."

Hugh was born in Saxony, later becoming prior of the monastery of St. Victor in Paris. In his day he was a leading mystical writer and renowned lecturer. The above saying focuses on the nature of Divine Love and its seemingly inherent paradoxes. Let's take them one by one.

Hugh suggests that the fullness of Divine Love is totally focused on each individual as if they were the only human being to have ever lived in their space-time world. Such a thought is mind blowing in its sheer simplicity. The Creator, Source of all Being, is totally focused on me as an individual, like an energy packed laser cutting through thick steel.

How then can we resist the power of such a Love?

The answer is simple: We can't. Our ego arrogance may suggest that we can, but in reality we're just deluding ourselves. Whether in this life or the next it will conquer us by its boundless mercy.

Yet such a Divine Love isn't private. Its devastating effect on each of us will flow out to others, just as a river flows into the ocean. Others will sense it by our very presence. Divinity will permeate our persona like water filling a sponge.

We religious folk are very wary of subjective feelings due to our programming by teachers who themselves are often frigid to the Divine approach. Easier to read a Holy book than open oneself to the Divine touch. Yeshua claimed that He would manifest Himself to His followers through the gift of Holy Breath/Spirit. Interestingly the Greek word translated *manifest* can mean *to be picked up by the human senses, to be experienced bodily*.

Divine Love is experienced in our aloneness, in our sense of isolation in a cosmos without meaning. The Linus blanket security of group identity provides a poor substitute. To be truly alone, we must be comfortable with our own presence and enjoy being in our own skin.

Tragically many spiritual seekers don't, eventually becoming pew fodder for those who promise to dispense God like a market trader. Yet, paradoxically, true mystics can relate well to their community. They may not be religious joiners or preacher junkies but they're organically joined to the whole of God's family, indeed to the whole human race. Their experience of Divine Love, contrary to popular opinion, doesn't make them exclusive, unlike the majority of fanatical practitioners of sectarian asceticism.

As a mathematics teacher, I taught my pupils that if a finite cake was shared between an infinite number of people then they'd each receive an infinitely small crumb, a particle so small in fact that it wouldn't actually exist. So where then did the totality of the cake's essence go?

Not surprisingly, I received lots of blank looks from my puzzled pupils in response to such a mind boggling puzzle. Thankfully Divine Love doesn't follow the laws of mathematics. It can be shared between mankind's billions but not be diminished in any way. We needn't be afraid of giving such Love away for it appears to follow the rules of Quantum Physics. If we give it away, it grows and multiplies within, surely the message of Yeshua's miracle feedings in the Gospel accounts. Like an exercised muscle, its dynamic power grows within us as we reach out to others, not initiated by a religious guilt complex but as a reflex response to Divine intimacy.

The Divine Father lies outside the boundaries time, hence His ever present Love can never run out during our earthly sojourn. It's as fresh today as it was at the creation of time and will stretch to the end of time and beyond.

Hugh of St. Victor certainly perceived some of the deepest mysteries of Divine Love. I mischievously suspect that he experienced such a Love in spite of his undoubted theological and philosophical expertise.

6

Ruysbroeck (1293-1381)

"Pay your debt. Love the Love that ever loves you."

Perhaps one of the greatest medieval European mystics, Ruysbroeck dedicated his life to the study of theology up to his fiftieth year. The second half of his life saw him unexpectedly retire to a forest hermitage with a few close friends. Here, the one time theologian remained for the rest of his days. In this second spiritual phase of his life, Ruysbroeck became a contemplative and a mystical counsellor.

What a short but deeply profound saying we have here. There's no talk of religious duty; Sunday observance or any other form of will- engineered piety. Instead, we're gently encouraged to return to the Divine the Love that He's already poured out on us.

Yet the term 'pay your debt' scares me a little. Why? After many years of 'debt paying' religious activity, I now believe that the human race has always stood debtless before its Source. Surely Ruysbroeck is trying to emphasise the supremacy of Divine Love and its role in the 'circle of life'.

Neither religious believers nor non believers can produce Divine or 'agape' Love; a Love that asks for nothing in return. Unless we're spiritually rewired by an encounter with such a Love, we can't produce such an ego-less outpouring. All we're asked to do is receive the flow of Love and pass it on, in the same way it was given i.e. freely. Yeshua claimed that as we let the Father's Love flow out towards others that in reality we'd be returning it to Him.

We must be careful not to be deceived by religious guilt in our love for God or our fellow man. Paralysing guilt or debilitating shame isn't involved in this cyclical process. Instead, it's the circular free flow of Spirit that Ruysbroeck is talking about; the water of Life that completes its own Divine circuit.

On this Easter Sunday, one of the most religiously celebrated days of the year, I wonder if our zealous devotion to Yeshua is guilt driven or a reflex response to Divine touch and intimacy. Like a determined Lover, God is seeking such intimacy with a broken humanity. Surely that's what life is all about.

7

The unknown author of 'The Cloud Of Unknowing' (14th Century)

"Lift up your heart to God with a meek stirring of love, and mean Himself and none of His goods."

We return once more to the mysterious writings of the unknown monk responsible for the 'Cloud of Unknowing'. There's a lot of wisdom contained in his short statement relating to contact with the Divine.

I don't know about you, but I'm tired of being encouraged by professional Christians to seek after God when, in fact, they're enthusiastically pointing me in the direction of their particular God box. Thankfully God doesn't do boxes so it's a complete waste of time looking for Him there. How, then, do we go about making contact with the Divine? In the above saying, our medieval monk suggests *lifting up our hearts* to God. Such simple advice sounds extremely pious but what does it actually mean? Here's a few thoughts based on my own chequered experience.

Paradoxically, I've discovered that the easiest time to *lift up my heart* to God is when I'm at rock bottom, at the end of my proverbial, spiritual rope, when I feel like undergoing a dramatic conversion to atheism. When I normally try to *lift up my heart,* its usually weighed down by so many psychological attachments that it rapidly falls straight back to earth. When I'm in a dark hole, wrestling with the pain of my broken attachments, I find, surprisingly, that Divine Presence draws very close, offering the spiritual lift required. In reality, even the act of seeking the Divine is His gift to us in such situations.

When we're feeling on top of things and perform the required religious gymnastics, God is often no-where to be seen. Dare I say it, but He seems to take an almost perverse delight in hiding from His friends when they seem to have it all together. That's why I honestly believe the Divine Father doesn't bother turning up for many traditionalist or trendy New Church services. There's a distinct lack of Presence at such staged events as His children skip merrily through their weekly God routine. It certainly bores me and I imagine that it bores Spirit, who'd rather draw alongside an alcoholic who's about to end his pain by jumping off a nearby bridge.

This *lifting of the heart* then, is a gracious gift granted when we voluntarily or involuntarily let go of all we place our security in; when all our little psychological Linus blankets are Divinely removed one by one. *Meekness* and its accompanying *stirring of love* instinctively know that the religious game is up; a demanding pastime that we need no longer play. When the plastic, mask inducing, sacred act is finally flushed down the religious toilet, Spirit is free once again to complete the psychic Love circuit, to reconnect us with the Divine Source.

One problem remains though. Whilst at the bottom of our darkest hole we're generally desperate for God to *do* something rather than simply comfort us with Presence. We're so programmed by society's quick fix that we perceive God as our Fixer when we run out of ideas and straight into trouble. Even the commonly perceived view of Yeshua as Saviour, can reflect this shallow type of somewhat infantile thinking. Let's not forget that the Galilean's ministry goal was no less than the restoration of a mature intimacy between Divinity and His estranged humanity.

Thankfully, Divine Love does pour out various gifts upon us. He just can't help Himself due to the fruit of His *agape* nature; the out-flowing of *favour* to believers and unbelievers alike. Yet He won't leave us in such a blessed state if we begin to draw our security from such gifts. God *passionately* desires communion with us and will wait patiently for us, our lifetime if needs be, to drop all our psychological attachments.

Seen in this light, all of life's experiences can only result in us falling deeper into the Divine and out of illusion, religious or otherwise. Such a dramatic change in our thinking removes so much self-induced stress out of daily living. As medieval mystic Lady Julian of Norwich proclaimed *'All is well, all shall be well and all manner of things shall be well'*. Like an exhausted puppy, resting peacefully on its master's lap, we can even now, rest in the healing wholeness of Divine Presence.

8

Fenelon (1651-1715)

"Let God act."

What a short but dynamic saying from Archbishop Fenelon who served at the ostentatious Versailles court of Louis XIV of France. Despite being surrounded by such a royal bunch, Fenelon was a deeply spiritual man who doubled up as spiritual director to Madame Guyon, the famous French mystic.

I thought I'd start, not with Fenelon's statement, but, if I may, with one of my own, believing that Fenelon's statement flows out of what I'm about to say.

"Let God be."

Our world is filled with multitudes of, what I frankly call, *zealous God botherers*, an army of little helpers who believe that the Divine can't save the world if they don't give Him a helping hand. *'Go into all the world and make disciples of all nations'* is the solitary proof text that generates such frantic activity among the often ant-like colony of religious believers. Busyness is interpreted as a sign of authentic faith and obedience, relegating the Divine to a slightly under powered deity who requires human effort, sweat and self-sacrifice to achieve His dream of world redemption.

We're told, *'Of course the Divine could handle it all Himself but He's a big hearted God who shares His mission with us.'* However, on closer inspection, it appears that God has handed the whole project into human hands and gone off for a 2000+ year siesta. I'm afraid that, after years on the religious treadmill, I can no longer believe in such a Divine Being, one who appears to be little more than a projection of the much revered Protestant work-ethic.

When a small child tries to annoy a sleeping pet, an impatient parent often implores *'Let it be'.* In similar fashion, we believers often pester the Divine so much with our long prayers, hypnotic worship songs, so-called good teaching, candles and incense that He doesn't get a chance to break through into our tunnel visioned consciousness. Let me humbly suggest that we give God some *Divine space* to do what He does best; the wooing of mankind in His own way and in His own time.

With this in mind let's now look at the good Archbishop's suggestion:

"Let God act"

How do we let God act? Indeed how does He act? To answer these two important questions let me introduce two radical ideas.

Firstly, let's stop being religious in order to help God out; Spirit Source doesn't need our two cents worth of sour-faced piety. Who are we trying to impress but our fractured, love-starved egos? *'Look, Daddy God, see how faithful I've been'* is a wounded child's cry for recognition and affirmation.

We've probably suffered such *primal wounding* of our self-worth at the hands of our imperfect parents, who inadvertently dispensed the trauma of conditional love from time to time during our upbringing. As adults, we even try out our resultant survival techniques on the Divine. Thankfully, He ignores them all, whilst weeping the precious tears of unconditional love over us in our brokenness.

Once we disengage from our comforting but fruitless piety plays, we can genuinely encounter Divine Love for perhaps the first time on our spiritual journey. The human practice of religious observance, particularly the zealous variety, is, indeed, often a cry *for Love* and not the response *to Love*. One who's encountered such an unconditional Love will, contrary to popular opinion, be shockingly non-religious; not irreligious, but in some unusual way, Divinely normal. The prototype of such a rewired or *born from above* humanity has been the Nazarene, Yeshua, who gloriously reflected the non-religious confidence of God's own Being.

Secondly, once we relinquish our anxious programme of spiritual gymnastics, how does the Divine then do His work? The answer is simple, yet deeply profound. *Holy Breath/Spirit itself* releases Divine Love to our lost and fractured world. Awakening to this radical realisation, we automatically become earthen channels for this ever rushing *agape* flow of Life.

Everything that is of value originates in Spirit before manifesting in the realm of matter. Indeed, all matter is a manifestation of our Creator Source, like the suns rays are to the Sun itself. All, so-called, *spiritual work* is simply the act of letting such a Spirit flow.

If we attempt to capture the essence of a river by catching some of its fast flowing water in a bucket, we've missed the whole point of its nature and purpose. Likewise, we pilgrims are placed on this wonderful planet Earth, to be carried along by Spirit-River's power, not to religiously domesticate it. Such an attempt at domestication is the essence of all sacred observance and thankfully, one that's bound to fail.

Way Beyond The Blue

> *We must not be discouraged by our ~~many~~ faults, for children fall frequently.*
> — St. Therese of Lisieux

Francis De Sales (1567-1622)

"Well my poor heart, here we are, fallen into the ditch which we had made so firm a resolution to avoid."

Francis De Sales suffered a pretty rough time of it during his relatively short faith walk. Firstly, his worldly wise father strongly disapproved of him entering the priesthood at age 26. Secondly, Francis was later appointed Bishop of Geneva but never got to preach in the city's great Catholic cathedral. This latter frustration was the responsibility of the famous Reformation theologian John Calvin who'd declared Geneva a Protestant city-state that didn't embrace those of the *other side*.

Francis must have had a fairly good sense of humour for there is something slightly comical about his response in the above saying. Perhaps it's a bit of self-deprecation uttered with tongue firmly in cheek. There's nothing that we religious folk love better than striving to be holy. It's almost an obsession for an orthodox believer. Many have gone to great lengths to try to earn the illusional Divine brownie points.

Thankfully those of a Protestant background, like myself, don't get into the self-flagellation pastime or I'd have a back full of bloodied scars. However, Protestant Christians do try to *overcome the flesh* in many creative but equally painful ways. A zealous religious group, I once belonged to, held its annual week of prayer and fasting in early January; probably the coldest and most depressing month of the Northern Irish year.

I guess we thought God would be more impressed with us fasting in cold conditions rather than the wet balmy days of the typical Ulster summer. As stoical warriors of faith, we were encouraged to eat, or should I say, drink soup without *bits* in it, such as a renegade pea or mischievous lentil.

Incidentally, on completion of the week's fast many of us youthful, alpha males made straight for a fast food joint, swopping the emptiness of our pietistic stomachs for the fleshly delights of a double-cheeseburger. Such is the foolishness of extreme religious enthusiasm.

Francis, in his above statement, is pointing out the ultimate weakness of human nature, even that of an apparently sincere God seeker. The stoical will has been set like flint towards *holiness* but the fragile soul has ended up in a ditch that he'd planned to avoid. Perhaps a case of what we fear coming to pass?

I love Francis's response though; he doesn't turn the penitential rack another notch and try harder. Instead, he wisely suggests picking himself up, honestly acknowledging his fall and getting back on the God Way. Francis clearly understood that the Divine Father is not some kind of belligerent quality controller, but a constantly loving Presence; one who smiles and guides us on our way after our ego's feeble, religious attempt at *being good*. Surely the Divine Source is far more interested in communion than supposed goodness.

Righteousness, for a Jew like Yeshua, wasn't a case of cold morality but an enjoyable state of restored harmony within close personal relationships. The Nazarene went so far as to flesh out His somewhat shocking take on the Divine in His frequent visits to sinners' parties. Religious virtue, or rather, *perceived* religious virtue is one of the greatest obstacles to experiencing the intimacy of Divine Presence. Apparently the *good living* religious types didn't enjoy being around Yeshua; the *sinners*, on the other-hand, seemed to thrive on it, loving to sit around listening to His little God stories.

Why?

The answer is simple; they'd no pietistic credit rating to block the flow of communion freely offered by a forgiving God. The religious observers, on the other hand, possessed their own hard earned virtue score, the result of much sacred sweat. They'd have had to flush it down the drain in order to get in touch with the Divine Presence as earthed in Rabbi Yeshua. Sadly, they weren't willing to do so and neither are we when we chalk up a few gold stars in God's service.

Thankfully, the Divine ignores all our religious baggage, focusing instead on the heart, the centre of our being, the sacred space within where encounter with Him is possible. So let's not be too hard on ourselves when our religious intentions come crashing down. If we fall asleep while trying to perform our religious duties, let's not beat ourselves up. If we swear at our boss and blow our holy image, let's not panic; let's just admit that we blew it and let the Divine Father dust us off before once more setting us back on the Way.

Finally, my friend Wayne Dunn suggests that there are two ditches into which we can fall on our God journey:

To the left we have the *anything goes* ditch. Life is short and to hell with it. Every passion is satisfied but the destructive downward spiral continues until we lie powerless at rock bottom, a prisoner to our insatiable desires and appetites.

To the right we have the *religious* ditch with its earned piety and repeated refusal of the Divine's unconditional Love. It's a ditch of sacred superiority in the guise of humility and self sacrifice.

So which ditch is the deepest?

Well, in light of my own past experiences, I suspect that

religious ditches win hands down. Ego produced piety is surely the most difficult mind defence that Spirit has to contend with on our journey Home.

The Divine has already forgiven us for the waywardness of our unawareness, so let's not treat ourselves too harshly. The second great commandment that Yeshua endorsed was, *"Love your neighbour as your Self"*. On close examination, many of us don't seem to know how to love our Self. Surely it's about time to follow Francis' advice and start today?

10

John Martin Sahajananda (born 1955)

"Jesus manifests a new level of consciousness, the consciousness of the kingdom of God according to which both the just and the unjust need conversion, need to discover their eternal being."

John Martin Sahajananda, is a Camaldolese monk at the Shantivanam Christian Ashram in South India, having been a close disciple of Father Bede Griffiths, a Benedictine monk and founder of the unusual community. Martin isn't a stereo-typical Christian monk since he brings an Eastern perspective to the sayings of Yeshua that most Western mystics miss.

Let's examine the above saying which takes a little getting used to for those of us steeped in Western religious thought. Its profundity lies in its radical dismissal of the dualistic world view of Christianity, one that predominates in the Greek influenced beliefs and practices of the Catholic and Protestant faiths .

Martin claims that Yeshua turned the concept of the

Kingdom of God upside down in first century Palestine. A revolution against Rome was expected by prophetically orientated Jews to be imminent. After all, hadn't their God, Yahweh, promised to send a military Saviour-King, known as Messiah or Anointed One, to lead the rebellion against the Beast of Rome.

Today, most Christians reckon that the Jews of Yeshua's time completely misinterpreted their ancient prophecies regarding the Messiah, believing instead that the Nazarene came to die as a Suffering Servant, One who redeemed the world. We could spend many hours exploring that particular interpretation but let's focus instead on what Yeshua was trying to communicate when referring to *The Kingdom of God*.

Clearly, Yeshua didn't share the conventional God-consciousness of his average Jewish listener. To them ,Yahweh lived way outside their daily experience, a transcendent deity who only manifested Himself in the Jerusalem Temple, behind a big curtain, in a dark, somewhat eerie room, known as the Holy of Holies. Yeshua thought otherwise. He talked to His disciples of finding a hidden treasure, a pearl of great price that would turn their lives upside down; pictorial hints of the secret Kingdom.

Why the discovery of hidden or lost objects to describe such a much sought God realm? The answer's so simple that traditional Christianity has long overlooked it. The Kingdom is and always has been resident in the human heart, the last place we spiritual seekers expect to find it. A Divine spark covered by the tangled clutter of our desire controlled consciousness.

Martin suggests that a *conversion* is required to rediscover this Divine consciousness or Kingdom within; not a moral conversion that claims to clean up a life but a much more radical change; an *awakening* from the deep sleep of ignorance. Thankfully, a higher state of consciousness is the liberating result of such an *awakening*, not the adoption of new religious dogma or practices, but a radical new way of perceiving the world, others and, most importantly, *oneself*. I believe such an awakening to be totally God initiated.

What then is to be our response to such a Love invasion?

Simply to ride the Divine flow once our internal spirit spark has been reignited. The life of God now reverberates deep within the psyche, like the roar of a car engine following the connection of jump-leads to a flat battery. One can never again see oneself, or indeed humanity, in the same light.

Perhaps the most shocking, resulting revelation is to discover that the Divine is neither angry nor wrathful with fallen humanity. Instead, Divinity manifests Himself as an unconditionally loving Presence. Such a change of paradigm shocks the long-established religious mindset and no wonder, for it renders all sacred, guilt-reducing games redundant.

Martin suggests that both those, with and without, religious virtue need such a *conversion* or *internal awakening*. Can therefore, the religious devotee, whose religion is externally based somewhere *way out there*, really claim to have experienced an authentic *conversion*?

Could this be the reason why alcoholics in the gutter may undergo life-changing, spiritual awakenings rather more quickly than regular pew sitters or good upstanding citizens? The former have very little to hang on to whilst the latter pride themselves on their *good* reputations.

Both sets of humanity need the Divine Light to reveal itself within. When our terrified, fractured psyches finally surrender their vice-like grip, such an empowering Light can, perhaps for the first time, project itself onto the screen of our human consciousness.

So what is this inner Divine spark?

Traditionally Christians have believed that Holy Breath/Spirit comes to dwell within the individual penitent at *conversion*. However, what if the Divine Interface was there all along, resident in our internal spark of spirit? Is Martin suggesting this inner point of Divine contact to be, none other than, our essential self, the very essence of our *I am-ness?* I believe so. Surely Divine Presence prefers to reside in such an authentic location rather than in the imposter, social-self realm of ego as programmed by our outer world.

Unfortunately, *Self* and *I* are somewhat taboo within mainline Christianity where they're often synonymous with Paul's, the *flesh,* his oft quoted personification of enmity against the Divine. However, have we got it all wrong? Could our inner Holy of Holies actually be our *I*, the spirit point of contact with the great *I Am*, the Abba God of Yeshua? *Our "interior castle", our soul.*

The spiritual writer, Anthony De Mello, while addressing a somewhat pietistic audience of priests and nuns, claimed that the most important question that we can ask ourselves isn't *'Does God exist?'* or *'Who is Jesus Christ?'* but rather, *'Who am I?'.* I believe that the Indian priest hit on something very profound in this seemingly shocking, if not downright sacrilegious, assertion.

Who are you? Who am I?

Perhaps we need to start all over again by letting our personal religious history drop to the ground like an old well-worn cloak? Are we trying to wear a spiritual garment well past its sell-buy date? Is this what Yeshua meant by being *born from above*? Indeed, can our current God concepts be blocking a further experience of God? May Spirit Breath within, lead us further into our consummated union with Divine Love.

Imago Dei

11

Madame Guyon (1648-1717)

"May I hasten to say that the kind of prayer I am speaking of is not a prayer that comes from your mind. It is a prayer that begins in the heart; prayer that comes from the heart is not interrupted by thinking."

Madame Guyon was a most unusual candidate for her role as a French mystic. Widowed at 28, following a deeply unhappy marriage, she was imprisoned by the authorities for seven years in response to her supposedly heretical writings. Guyon was a Quietist whose views of an interior life threatened the religious establishment of her time. Her critics claim that she was obsessed by the suffering she'd endured throughout her tragic life, yet I believe she reveals great spiritual awareness, especially in her quotation above.

Madame Guyon claims that there are two kinds of prayer: that which originates in the mind and that which ascends to the Divine from the human heart. Western Christianity has always been extremely mind-centred, due, in part, to its absorption of Greek philosophy in its formative years. Such Greek thought has, I believe, reinterpreted the sayings and message of Yeshua, a Middle Eastern Jew with a Semitic take on the Divine.

The development of theology and the belief-centred religious tradition can be traced back to this and other intellectual influences. In contrast, mysticism, both Jewish and Christian, is another branch of spirituality where the subjective, feeling part of Divine engagement takes precedence over the thought filled mind. No longer is analytic reason the control centre of religious experience but *the heart* or *spirit*. Eastern religions such as Hinduism and Buddhism also incorporate strong mystical traditions that strongly encourage the bypassing of the limiting conscious mind.

May I suggest that genuine prayer flows, like a bubbling spring, from the deepest part of our being and can in fact be wordless. Perhaps this is what Paul of Tarsus, no mean mystic himself, proposes when he describes the *spirit* groaning within us.

Can words and language actually block the sense of communion between us and the Divine?

I believe so. Words and their companion language are simply conceptual manifestations that have controlled human behaviour since ancient times. Have we over-relied on conceptual Christianity instead of the intuitive, sensory faith that many of the mystics through the ages enjoyed? I believe the fruit of such a conceptual base to be sadly self evident in the rivalrous divisions within most modern religious expressions.

Unfortunately, a deep suspicion of intuitive based religious experience is often programmed into the new Christian convert by those with an interest in promoting an intellectual version of faith, namely the professional clergy. *Surely we Yeshua followers need a major paradigm shift in order to help us experience the Presence of spirit.*

Modern psychology, the study of the fragmented soul, has already proven the complex mind-body link. Can we not go one step further by promoting the mystical body-spirit link. Ancient religions, especially those of indigenous peoples have long recognised such a vital link between our *physical manifestation* and our essential timeless essence .

Is this what Madam Guyon had in mind? Can spirit communicate with Spirit without the need for language and the adjudication of the conscious mind?

American neuroscientists have recently demonstrated that the unusual religious phenomenon of *tongues speaking* or *glossolalia,* bypasses the traditional language centre of the human brain. In other words, such a phenomenon isn't a learned or mimicked activity.

Could such a psycho-spiritual activity be a primal communion between body (vocal chords) and Divine Spirit?

As followers of Yeshua why don't we step out and explore alternative forms of prayer, more in-tune with these amazing earthen vessels that we've been given? It would surely help overthrow the ego dictatorship that so often rules through our deeply driven consciousness.

Let's give it a go!

> *Spiritual evolution is demanding, often frightening, always life-altering. It means* Way Beyond The Blue *letting go of ideas that no longer serve us. It means taking our power, becoming our own spiritual authority. It means being a finder, not a seeker.*
>
> — Jan Phillips

Gerhard Tersteegen (1697-1756)

"You don't need to search for God; you have only to realise Him."

Gerhard Tersteegen wasn't a typical European mystic in that he didn't subscribe to the Catholic faith. Indeed, Tersteegen wasn't even a member of any Protestant denomination, believing all man-made groupings to be irrelevant to spiritual progress. He was, however, described by his fellow Germans as a member of the little *Friends Of God* movement, a loose grouping that encouraged Christian Pietism throughout the pretty godless eighteenth century state.

These *Friends of God* believed in an individual experience of Divine Love that would mainly manifest itself through works of charity among the poor. Tersteegen himself worked as a simple ribbon-weaver for most of his adult life, with many spiritual seekers coming to him for instruction and inspiration. His devotional influence spread far beyond Germany's borders with both John and Charles Wesley touched by his inspired hymns.

Tersteegen's little saying is profoundly simple in its message. Let's have a look at it in two parts:

Firstly, Tersteegen suggested that an individual doesn't have to seek out the Divine. Rather, he informs us, the Divine actively seeks us. Here then is a somewhat controversial thought; religion tries to seek God while spirituality recognises that such a search is pointless and indeed, ultimately self defeating.

Do we perceive ourselves to be religious people? If so, what qualifies us for such a label? Is it our checklist of conceptual God beliefs or our rigorous, sacred practices such as prayer or scripture reading? Is it our membership of a formal faith group known as a church? What exactly does define a religious person? It's an extremely difficult and complex question to answer. Many folk confidently claim that they're not religious but Christian, believing that they've left nominal, works based religion behind for reality as revealed in Yeshua the Nazarene i.e. Jesus Christ.

Having worn that particular tee-shirt myself for many years, I couldn't or wouldn't admit that I was, in fact, an *extremely religious* Christian. Everyone outside my sect or belief system was clearly religious whereas I, and my fellow devotees, were simply just Christian.

I'm afraid my youthful, simplistic, black and white mind-set was a delusion of the highest order. There is no doubting it; I was extremely zealous as evidenced by my various, ascetic devotions toward my illusionary Christ,

God and, indeed, my particular sect. So blinded was I to my prevalent psycho-spiritual state, that Divine Love had to lovingly, but firmly, cold turkey me off such a religious asceticism via the painful route of sceptical agnosticism before I could re-encounter Him. We may be seekers after God but are we not very religious ones at that? If so, then let's stop immediately. It will be the first liberating step in the Divine finding us.

Secondly, Tersteegen suggests an alternative approach to discovering the Divine; that of *realising* Him. It sounds so simple but what on earth does the mystical weaver mean? A few illustrations may give us a hint as to how to come to this radical realisation.

In the movie *Finding Nemo* the eager little fish is frantically swimming along when he stops and asks this vexing question of his fellow sea farers.

"Can you tell me where I can find the ocean?"

We're so like the childlike, but nevertheless, ignorant Nemo, in our lack of awareness. Surrounded by the object of his frantic search, the poor little fish didn't *realise* or *know* it. Paul of Tarsus, quoting the Greek poet Aratus, reminds the sceptical Athenians that *'In Him we live and move and have our being'*. It would appear then that we're already *in God* and perhaps, even more startling, that He's somehow *within us*.

Recently, I've been having a recurring dream which at

first was proving difficult to interpret. In it I was back at my old boyhood school, prior to sitting an important examination. I hadn't prepared for the academic ordeal ahead and was having a discussion with my teacher regarding my lack of preparation. The terrifying conviction that I was on the brink of failing the dreaded examination filled me with deep dread. Suddenly, in the midst of such surreal angst, a *revelation* or *realisation* came to me. I was no longer an adolescent schoolboy but an adult who'd already passed the examination many decades before. The tangible sense of utter relief was completely overwhelming in the dream, prompting me to immediately inform the teacher that I wouldn't be sitting the examination. With no reason to stay, I then saw myself confidently march out through the cell-like examination-hall door. This particular dream contains a variety of lessons for me on many psychic levels but here's one in line with our present discussion.

The examination is the religious quest for the Divine. I panic, believing myself to be deeply inadequate for such a task, like an Arthurian knight desperately trying to find the much sought Holy Grail. The teacher represents the religious authority figures who inform me that I must sit the examination, follow the traditional religious route, in a disciplined and ordered manner.

My sudden dream awareness of being an adult represents the acceptance of my individuated Self, the centre of my inner Being. The *realisation* that I've already passed the examination is the revelation that the Divine and I have already encountered one another many years previously. <u>Indeed, outside space-time there has never been a *time* when we were apart. Divine Love has always been there, cradling me in its eternal arms.</u>

Realising God then, is a growing awareness of the surrounding Divine Presence that permeates the detailed minutiae of our conscious existence, while paradoxically dwelling in the very depths of our psyche. Like a fearful child waking from a devilish nightmare, we'll discover the warm, waiting comfort of the Parental Presence. Why don't we simply stop beating ourselves up with religious striving and relax back into the Divine stillness, the Home in which we are meant to dwell?

we were made
By Love
For Love
To Love
Father Jay, 2.3.19

Part Two

Mystical Musings

13

Hot Or Cold Spirituality?

I'm sitting here on my swing-seat enjoying the view and basking in the beautiful May sunshine. The cold weather fronts of the past six months finally seem to be releasing their icy grip on the battered British psyche. These welcome new temperatures are definitely the ones designed for personal meditation!

Is it a coincidence that all four major world religions were birthed in countries with very hot climates? I tend to think not for the following reasons.

In hot, sweat-inducing climates the frantic work ethic of the Northern Europeans psyche is a non-starter. Who could possibly keep such a frantic pace of existence going in all that heat? The indigenous peoples of these oven-like climates often appear lazy to us stress-bunny Westerners; *good for nothings,* as my workaholic dad would have described them. Yet from among such peoples came the various Divine revelations that, even today, still impact much of the world's population. How come?

The peoples of such climes live slowly, perceiving life as

a long journey, not the 100 metres sprint that most of us Westerners imagine it to be. Is there a link between this slow pace of life and the origins of their Divine revelations? I think so!

Such revelations came to apparently chosen individuals during periods of, what our English weather forecasters would describe as, *high temperatures*. The Jewish, Christian and Muslim holy writings are full of unexpected encounters with *the Other*. For example poor old Abram sitting under the shade of a Canaanite tree when he spots three angelic visitors approaching.

When the body slows down an openness to Divine transcendence occurs via the portal of the Transpersonal Self or human spirit. Surely this is why many of us find Spirit during illness or hospitalization when our exhausted body surrenders its manic desire to stoically keep going in the emotional rat race. During cold temperatures our bodies try to conserve heat and may I suggest that our rigid egos try to conserve our social identity, our personal status quo. Periods of intense cold are not times for spiritual revelation; instead they shock us into survival mode. Like little squirrels we scurry around trying to stash enough *psychic stuff* to get us through the spiritual winter. Materialism thrives in the autumn of our lives, as we scamper though the forests of desire seeking a nest egg that will carry us to the doors of death.

The Indian sub-continent has produced the deeply

meditative religions of Hinduism and Buddhism. Where did the Buddha encounter his much sought after enlightenment? Yes, under a Bodhi tree. Maybe we followers of Yeshua should collectively meet in a forest or individually sit under our own personal prayer tree. Give the pews and air-conditioned buildings a miss at least during the summer months.

Another thought strikes me regarding high temperature lands. The need for water. In hot climates water is the number one priority. Middle Eastern analysts reckon that the regions next war will not be about oil but water. The rivalling countries aren't so much land grabbers as water grabbers. Behind much violence is the craving for water; no water, no life.

Scriptures of all traditions abound in water imagery. Yeshua promised Divine water that would eradicate the Samaritan woman's thirst for acceptance that she'd attempted to quench through numerous male attachments. Prophets and seers saw water as a metaphor for Spirit Source. As the human body needs clean water so the sensitive psyche requires the energy flow of Divine Love channelled through Holy Breath. Simple but profound.

Have I given up the materialistic buzz produced by the rat race to sit under my personal *meditation tree?* Have I drunk of Divine Presence in its cooling shade? In the hot climate of Palestine, Yeshua was big into trees and water. *Am I?*

14

Rivers & Buckets ~ Part 1

Rivers pop up everywhere in religious scriptures probably because they're sources of water, that is itself symbolic of Spirit. They're everywhere – in Eden, the God Garden, right the way through to the New Jerusalem, the God City. What is it about this particular imagery that places it in so many holy writings or scriptures?

Well, water, if you'll excuse the pun, is essential to life, especially for those inhabiting the barren and often dry lands of the Middle East. Remember no water = no life. I want to develop this thought a bit further, if I may, by exploring the idea of flowing water, i.e. our entitled *River* above.

May I suggest that you read the following short story before taking a few minutes to tune into your inner Voice. Ask Spirit to reveal anything that He wishes to communicate to you. In the meditative silence you may become aware of pictures, thoughts or even bodily sensations breaking through into your conscious mind. In the next chapter I'll share my own thoughts on the little parable.

Once upon a time a small group of people found themselves travelling by raft along a very powerful river that snaked its way through a varied and yet extremely exciting terrain. One minute they sailed in fairly calm waters, the next, a waterfall confronted them that threatened their very existence. The thing that excited the crew was their sense that the river was alive, full of movement and yet totally unpredictable. As they floated along, dodging the rapids that regularly came their way, the travellers noticed the fish that reassuringly swam alongside, also hearing the neighbouring bird song that drifted through the warm still air.

When the travellers tried to control their raft they'd end up in the brink, soaked to the skin. The only effective way to make progress was to trust the raft as the river's untamed waters carried them along. Their destination was a city, famous for its gold, that lay at the rivers end, as it merged with the Great Ocean.

After a few days, however, one or two of the crew decided that enough was enough! The river banks, with their rich vegetation, looked very appealing as a place where the travellers could rest. Eventually a vote was taken and the decision made. The raft would be hauled into a small quiet inlet on the riverbank and camp set up for the night. The travellers realised that water was essential to life and so, once camped, walked to the water's edge and captured some of the crystal clear river water in a few old rusty buckets. The ride on the river had been exhilarating but now they'd decided to rest, the buckets providing the perfect receptacle for the precious river water.

Next morning, after a sound night's sleep, the travellers decided to remain on the bank for another day, mesmerised by the surrounding sights and sounds of the countryside. The day's water was drawn from the nearby river and the rusty buckets given pride of place in the camp. A few days later, someone raised the idea of staying for good at the river's edge and building a simple settlement. Then they could have the best of both worlds! This novel suggestion was wholeheartedly and unanimously agreed upon by the travellers. After all they'd still be close to the river and could draw on its fast flowing water.

A month later, now enjoying the sumptuous fruit that grew on the river bank, the raft travellers had morphed into settlers. One evening, one of the party suggested that they should build a special place for the buckets due to their importance within the life of the fledgling community. The old raft was taken apart, plank by plank and its river-battered wood carefully prepared for its new use.

Next morning the settlers started upon their new project with great vigour. At the end of a laborious day, a small ornate building had been constructed and the freshly filled buckets placed on a gilded altar, for all to revere. That

Way Beyond The Blue

night the settlers partied until well past mid-night, celebrating the newly finished sanctuary for their 'beloved' buckets, the blessed containers of their daily water supply.

Awakening late the next morning, the keeper of the buckets lifted them from their sacred, resting place and walked enthusiastically down to the river's edge to draw water, as was his daily habit. What a shock awaited him! All that lay before him was a dry river bed. Not a drop of water in sight. The river had changed its course overnight, now flowing through a distant land, where a new bunch of travellers were queuing up to ride it as it flowed towards the city of gold. As the stunned bucket keeper stared into his empty buckets, a small tear gently slipped down his freshly blanched cheek. Paradise lost!

15

Rivers & Buckets ~ Part 2

I wonder what you thought of my little story *Rivers and Buckets* in the previous chapter. Was your response one of anger, bewilderment, plain boredom or an unexpected curiosity? The enchanting thing about Truth is that it sneaks up on us in many guises. Perhaps you've experienced a little momentary spark of illumination after meditating on the parable; perhaps not. Neither I, nor anyone else can dictate what Truth is. While in this earthbound state we can only share our personal perspective on it. Yours may be completely different to mine. With that limitation in mind I'll humbly offer you a few of my own insights into the watery tale.

Divine Spirit is like running water; never static, always teeming with life and bubbling with overflowing creative energy. Water wasn't created to sit in a bucket but to flow towards the ocean, where it evaporates into cloud, falls as rain, before returning as a river. Spirit will not, and indeed cannot, be contained in the vessel of human interpretation.

We humans were designed to live in a Spirit flow, to be carried by Spirit into the Divine Presence.

The wooden raft symbolises the frailty and vulnerability of our humanity carried along by the power of Spirit.

Paradoxically, following Spirit appears as a terrifying exercise to the ego, while being in Reality the safest and indeed only way to live.

If we try to control the raft of our lives we will ultimately fall in some unexpected way.

There exists an exciting camaraderie with other raft riders, but no-one is captain of the raft; only the River is in charge.

We can leave the raft lifestyle at any time by swapping the River for dry land and its promised security.

Initially, the decision to plump for security leads to rest and a new sense of control. However it doesn't last.

The River isn't totally abandoned but remembered in the illusory collection of its life flow in rusty buckets viz. our ultimately, futile attempt to contain its waters in our theological concepts.

The water in the buckets no longer constitutes the River; no movement = no River and hence no Life.

If left, the bucket water will turn stagnant, a breeding place for all sorts of harmful microbes. What was Life-giving in the River now becomes a source of ill-health and dis-ease; Spirit essence departs leaving toxic religion.

God concept buckets are eventually revered and given pride of place in a special sacred sanctuary; the Divine flow is exchanged for thought-filled ceremonies conceptualising the River.

A learned priestly class quickly emerges that attempts to bring a little of the River water to the recently settled *Community of the Rusty Buckets*.

No longer does anyone ride the River directly; the bucket keeper is paid to approach its banks and bring a few litres of still water back for the community's spiritual needs. An extremely gifted, well trained bucket keeper handles the God concept buckets for all the settled villagers. There's even talk of him publishing a book recounting his life with *The Buckets*. He's contemplating calling it *The Purpose Filled Bucket Life* with lucrative book tours already planned for Europe, Australia and the USA.

The River is extremely gracious, yielding up its clear water to the settlers for a period of time, waiting to see if they'll ride its rushing waters once more. The River, however, won't be contained or manipulated indefinitely. As the Bucket community sleeps, it mysteriously flows off in a new direction, fulfilling its desire to carry all trusting raft riders to the Great Ocean.

The *Bucket Community* have fond memories of bygone days when they rode the revivalist River; the Buckets are still as revered as ever on their sacred altar, but nowadays, water is found by cutting open the prickly cacti in the surrounding desert.

In my more pensive moments I want to be a raft rider until the day I drop. Don't you?

Dylan Morrison

16

Spiritual Ecosystems

Yesterday was a sun-drenched day, here in Lincoln, England, so my wife, Zan, puppy, Suki, and I set out for a much-needed walk in the nearby Nature Reserve. In the hot, summer sunshine, everything around us appeared to teem with Life-force and Divine energy.

The grey squirrels scampering along wooded paths, the blue dragon-flies hovering over silently still water, the greenest of green leaves blowing gently in the soft breeze at the apex of ancient trees; suddenly all seemed well with the world.

This marvelous little ecosystem conveyed deep mystery and yet a sense of worldly wholeness as we walked along by the edge of swan adorned lakes. No striving for the good things of life in this little natural world. Only the calm acceptance of Being, the wondrous and life-giving whole; each member celebrating its uniqueness in the rich collage of beauty and colour; each member devoid of ego, happy to play its role even if that's being eaten by a predator higher up the food chain. A multitude of individual species, filling the jig-saw like snapshot of Divine beauty.

It's all got me thinking. Is there a parallel spiritual ecosystem that reflects the ethereal Nature of Divine Mystery?

I believe there is, and it's called *Life*. This sea of joy and pain, in which we find ourselves immersed, throbs with Divine energy and generosity. Perhaps you disagree, suggesting instead that *The Church* is God's only ecosystem, isolated and surrounded by a dark, hostile world. I used to believe that too, but thankfully, no longer.

The Divinity that re-hijacked me, back in June 2004, now appears to have a much bigger heart than my previous experience of Him would have suggested. It's His world and always will be, the stage on which He directs the scripted human drama called Life.

As we march around the stage strutting our stuff and doing our thing, we foolishly believe that our free will is producing our one-man play. A dangerous delusion if ever there was one.

We're spirit beings fleshed out in this Divine Matrix known as *human existence*. Quantum scientists now suggest that, at a sub atomic level, our material world, including our all too earthly bodies are, in fact, complex manifestations of energy.

All energy is energy, suggesting an inherent Oneness of all matter. In other words, the harmony we experience while in the midst of Nature's beauty is no mere accident;

in some mysterious way we're birthed by the same Source, the same creative energy.

I've recently begun to ponder the inherent dualism within traditional Christianity - good and evil, God and the devil, heaven and hell etc. If all matter is essentially one, why not also the realm of spirit?

Perhaps you're already running for cover in order to arm yourself to the teeth with Biblical proof texts. There's no need to, for I know them all. Remember that for most of my youth I was a fighting fundamentalist with my big black Bible constantly at the ready for spiritual combat.

In our conservative Christian mindset, the dualism of believer and non believer subtly feeds our religious egos as we take refuge in the hothouse environment commonly known as the Church. We're the *saved* while anyone outside our sacred greenhouse is *unsaved* and ultimately deserving of the Divine bonfire. Dualism of the most hideous kind.

Let's be frank; the high fervour-inducing temperatures of our Christian hothouses promise a little taste of Heaven on Earth, but often end up producing wilted, waterless plants, much to the bewilderment of their sacred gardeners. The new batch of seedlings planted after a successful outreach are force fed the same menu of Biblical fertiliser, watered by a hyped up sense of Holy Breath and left to grow in the tropical temperatures of religious enthusiasm; all under the watchful eye of the resident spiritual horticulturist. Unfortunately history repeats itself, for the destructive doctrine of dualism is the dark foundation of the religious greenhouse.

I once met a guy called Tim who used to be a street anarchist prior to his dramatic conversion to Christianity. He stoically went along with the church thing for about six months while constantly bewildered at the society that he'd walked into; a greenhouse ecosystem that produced little genuine fruit or spiritual growth (i.e. love). Tim now lets the *real world* disciple him in the ways of Yeshua, his work of financing alternative spiritual grass roots projects being the fruit of this radical decision. I suspect that Tim may have inadvertently stumbled upon the inherent Unity of all things.

How then are we to live in the light of such a Unity? For my part, I'm trying not to label folk outside my present belief system, indeed expecting the Divine to communicate with me through anyone brought across my path. I attempt to listen for the Divine Voice in every circumstance that comes my way.

How has this changed my spiritual walk? Strange as it may seem I'm more than abundantly provided for; emotionally, materially and spiritually the Divine Spirit appears to have many more channels open through which to dispense Unconditional Love upon me and my family.

Many visitors will walk through my local Nature Reserve this weekend and see nothing. They'll be totally unaware of the joyous birdsong and the rich, warm earth beneath their feet.

Why don't we straight- jacketed followers of Yeshua let the Divine have His world back? How? By enjoying our Spirit-immersed walk through the vibrant ecosystem that we call *real life*.

17

Inner Peace

Are you interested in inner peace? I sure am, and have been since I first became aware of my internal angst at the tender age of twelve. Where does such angst come from? Why do I still want to search the depths of life's meaning, while most of my friends pretend they've found it, paddling around in the formulated shallows? Let's explore the whole self identity thing in this chapter.

My dear Christian friends and their pastor/priest overseers inform me that the dreaded three letter word *sin* is the primary cause of my angst. Alienation from a transcendent, holy God, One who can't bear to look on us falling short of His perfection, is the source of my perverted sense of aloneness, according to their formulaic, evangelical reasoning. The resulting gulf between us is so wide that Yeshua needs to act as a bridge between His God and me, a typical representative of wayward mankind.

I used to be fluent in all St. Paul's proof texts for this line of argument but unfortunately most of them have now slipped back into the recesses of my mind. What is it with we Yeshua followers and scripture verses anyway? I never could understand why many middle-class Christian homes in my Irish homeland were decorated with pretty little verse-tapestries all over their hallowed sitting room walls.

Anyway, depending on one's cultural framework, sin ranges from having a quick fag to being an extremely bloody mass murderer. Of course the more astute among us would proclaim, with an air of theological superiority, that those unfortunate misdemeanours are merely the fruit of the infamous sin tree.

Such a tree's poison lies in its deep root system; a rebellion against God that can only be solved by reckoning oneself dead to its insidious power through believing in the substitutionary atonement of Yeshua on the cross and asking for His Father's forgiveness. Everything will then be hunky dory as long as one does the decent Christian thing by conforming to the teachings and practices of the fellow believers whom God sends across your path.

In my own experience such a religious regime worked for a while but unfortunately my deep seated angst just point blank refused to go away. Indeed, at times it only seemed to get worse. How many Yeshua followers do you know, who, like me, are stressed out and on as many antidepressants as the next man? Why do so many professional clergy crack up or run off with their organists of either sex for a *better* life? Why do so many conscientious church goers eventually give up on the whole religious show by swopping their Sunday morning pew for a warm, cosy bed?

My own experiential theory is that, shockingly, extreme religious thinking can, if left unchecked, actually make our inner angst worse. Could it be that a lot of so-called unchurched *sinners* suffer less angst than their believing counterparts? Perhaps!

Most religious belief systems love *dualism*, indeed, they thrive on it. *'What,'* you may ask, 'is *dualism?'* Well simply it's black and white, God and the Devil, darkness and light, evil and righteousness, St Peter and Count Dracula - you name it. Indeed, we can probably fill a book with all the duelling dualisms that swirl around our dizzy consciousness. The bottom line is that our Western rationalism thrives on dualism and so surprisingly does the Church.

Strangely enough, the religions and philosophies of Eastern origin don't tend to buy into our dualistic view of reality; instead they're big into Unity or Oneness. Neuroscientists presently claim that the happiest man in the world is a French Buddhist monk. Just a coincidence? I think not. So who's right?

Yeshua certainly loved to talk about unity. *'I and the Father are One'*, *'You are in me and I am in you'* etc. John's mystical gospel is full of this kind of united Oneness talk. Have we missed the whole point of Yeshua's spirituality and message? I'll let you decide that for yourself.

Meanwhile let's backtrack to my angst. Psychologists of the psycho-synthesis variety claim that all our suffering stems from the fragmentation of the psyche or soul. Wired for unconditional love and empathy, our first experiences of such a splitting of the developing Self emanate from our parents, particularly our mothers.

No-one is perfect, and so my evolving sense of Me is, literally, halted in its infancy by the break down of empathy flowing from my frazzled mother; an often desperate lady who may be enduring a number of real off days. In order to survive these regular and often dramatic breaks in empathic Selfhood, we develop little survival sub-personalities to cope with the threatened pain of a terrible non-being.

These daring little darlings live within us for the rest of our lives, like the cast of a stage-play, each one called to perform his/her dramatic role when the appropriate threat of non-being occurs. Together this chequered company of actors comprise our 'Social Self', our public personality, often competing with each other for centre stage in the pin ball drama of our lives.

Our *spirit I* or *Essential Self* gazes down upon the twists and turns of the dramatic production and is amazed. What a stressful mess. Psycho-synthesis practitioners believe that the recognition and eventual reintegration of the actor sub-personalities will ultimately lead to a restored peace and wholeness, thereby setting free the psyche/soul to be all that God intended it to be. Such a reintegration of our maverick selves leads to a rich new union within, from which love and longed for Self acceptance can flow.

I believe that the mistaken Pauline dualism of flesh versus spirit causes much angst and pain within those spiritual seekers who desire the Holy Grail of inner peace. The more zealous the seeker, the more they engage in this unwinnable battle by ratcheting up psychic energy levels to repress and subdue the wrongly perceived *flesh* enemy.

However, by fighting our inner enemies or demons we paradoxically empower them. Welcome them into the growing community of our Self and the war is over. As a result, Divine Love flows, gifting us with all the empathic authentication that we require; we are now aware that we're no less than the sons and daughters of God. We can at last invite all of our inner demon sub-personalities to the internal Wedding Feast to celebrate the Union of *I* and the Divine.*

So let's resolve to ditch our religious, war-footing language, with its inner tensions and the often accompanying, physical sickness. After all we're followers of Yeshua, the Prince of Peace. If His peace isn't within then where is it? Give you Self a break. Welcome it with open arms. Ditch the so-called war on Self. You'll be pleasantly surprised at the results.

*Shadow work leads to the knowing that I am "love, loved & loving"... that I have always, already been enough, whole & holy in Him who Is within & without

18

Eden's Desire

I've been recently revisiting the old, Jewish, Creation story and its Utopian setting of Garden of Eden. Professor Richard Dawkins and his fellow new atheists would, I'm sure, pour scorn on me for taking such a infantile trip down mythical lane. Their reason for doing so is, I believe, quite clear. Mr Charles Darwin, and his evolutionary descendants, have over the last hundred and fifty years authored a new and much more Modernist take on the Genesis tale. One that has inspired God haters from around the globe to beat up on their poor misguided siblings who still cling to a Creator God.

Anyway, you'll be relieved to know that I'm not going to delve into the pros and cons of biological theory in this chapter; the simple reason being that I wasn't very good at it at school. I'm afraid that my Darwinian teacher didn't really take to me that much due to my teenage *Jesus Freak* persona. As a result, I tragically hid at the back of the classroom and learnt very little. Following on from my last chapter, 'Inner Peace', I'd much rather look at any lessons this little Gardening tale has to teach us about the psycho-spiritual human condition.

Firstly, it would appear that we're primarily here to enjoy a sense of Unity and Oneness with our Divine Source, each other and the world of Nature that we find ourselves immersed in. Each primeval evening, we're told, Spirit would take a purposeful stroll through Eden with the intention of bumping into and having a *yarn*, (as we Irish would put it), with his human handiwork.

It might sound a mite too pastoral for the city dwellers among us, but it still sounds good to me. A regular date with God where we neither had to fear, grovel nor attend a church, temple or mosque. Just a gentle stroll in Eden Park, around Paradise lake; not a whiff of religion nor self-sacrificial breast beating to be seen. Until their unfruitful downfall, our Adamic grandparents seemed to get along so well together, hand in glove you might say, even without the aid of a pre-marital Bible Course.

The animal world harmoniously agreed with Adam on their chosen names, being only too happy to leave him and the beautiful Eve off their lunch menu. Even the plants joined in the Divine Dance of Unity, with not a disruptive dandelion weed in sight. Oneness, yet diversity, to blow the mind; a Divine State indeed.

Secondly, something dynamically dysfunctional eventually weaved its way into this heady mix of bliss; a fast talking snake filled with desire. This poor old Serpent has, over the millennia, been identified with the ultimate God Nemesis, Satan, Lucifer, the Devil etc. Now maybe that's not fair on the snake nor indeed Satan but let's just say he was a big Serpent with an itchy urge. This mysterious, out-of-nowhere figure possessed a dark desire to screw up the whole Divine Unity thing.

Where did this desire come from? We're not told in the story, so maybe it's not important nor any of our business. Anyway, one thing's for sure; <u>the devious desire spread from snake to mankind by means of a simple but ultimately damaging question.</u>

'Has God said, "You will not eat of every tree in the garden"?'

How amazing. A hooked question and its subtle follow up were the oral transmitters of <u>misaligned desire</u>; igniting a spark of neediness within our otherwise happily ignorant, human ancestry. Such a skewed transfer of desire is at the heart of the human problem, according to our tale's Jewish author.

This shocking, but simple truth of desire transfer has been unmasked. What we consider to be our autonomous desire may, in fact, have its origin in a *significant other*; a model, whose *being* we want to possess. In infancy this transmitter role is played by our parents, their desires flowing into our empty, but crucially, open psyches, where they can take up residence for life.

Even the ultimate deaths of our parents don't automatically shift or expel these imported and oft imprisoning desires, as many of us have discovered to our cost. A friend of mine has a deep religious addiction, her father having been an alcoholic. Same desire, just a change of brand. Even in adulthood our childlike desire sponge is prone to soak up the desires of others. Beware of the charismatic man or woman with strong desire. They might just get under your skin.

Thirdly, what did our misguided ancestors desire? A big Golden Delicious or a Cox's Orange Pippin? I think not. The virulent desire was targeted at being *like* the Divine. A crazy attempt as the Adamic couple were already at One with the benign Garden stroller; the Spirit Breath that wafted around them in the cool of the day.

Our poor ancestors desired something that they already enjoyed. Now that's what I call a crafty con-job. That snake was good; very, very good. Somehow poor young A&E believed that they were missing out on something; Divinity or one of His amazing attributes.

The story goes that a *knowledge of good and evil* was the object of their new craving. In other words, their newly desired goal for acquisition was moral dualism, a profound psychic sense of right and wrong. This should shock us religious folk who consider morality a God thing. It's *not* – the snake lied.

Such a moral mindset can be simply summed up as follows: our views are *right* (and so God loves us) and yours are *wrong* (and so God will send you evil doers to a gnashing of teeth place - forever). What is this big addiction that we're all into - the Right and Wrong game? *'Dylan Morrison, you're right so Come on Down! John Doe, I'm afraid you're wrong so kindly leave the building and take the quickest route to hell'.*

In my forty five years of religious reading and study all that I've ended up with is theological knowledge, a handy little weapon that further fragments my community of neighbours, friends and, indeed, all mankind. A wonderful power play for the logic driven brain but not, I'm afraid, for the human spirit-heart.

Religious or spiritual head knowledge leads, not to *Inner Peace,* but rather inner and outward fragmentation, judgement, condemnation and, in many tragic cases, verbal or physical violence. The deadliest plague that mankind faces today is our knowledge of good and evil and, let's face it, religions of all varieties thrive on it; it is the air in which they breathe. Indeed, even the supposedly scientific new atheists thrive on it. It's everywhere.

Has Divine Source provided an escape route out of this domineering desire to be right? Can we walk in Oneness again with Spirit and our fellow man, in the cool of our days? I believe so.

Yeshua, was the man outside of desire. The model man who'd no desire to be *right* and no desire to exclude the *other*. Seen in this light, his life and death comprised a cosmic drama acted out for our benefit. A scapegoat victim buried in a Garden tomb. The resurrection claims of His

Way Beyond The Blue

early followers forcefully declare the rebirth of a fallen humanity; one reconciled and welcomed back into the Garden to walk with Holy Breath in the cool of the day. I love gardens. Don't you?

Fall not into the grip of desire, lest, like fire, it consumes your strength. A stubborn, obstinate soul destroys itself. Sirach 6:2,4

19

Go Man Go

Having recently been stuck down by laryngitis, listening to my own thick Ulster accent has unexpectedly given way to tuning into an even deeper Voice within. Here are a few of my resulting thoughts on why an encounter with Divine Love can often end up alongside a geographical relocation.

I reckon *God chasers* have always been riding their camels, chariots, horses or Cadillacs since the beginning of time. In the previous chapter, *Eden's Desire*, we noticed how, due to some subliminal Serpent desire transfer, the Divine could no longer walk with our Adamic prototypes in the cool of The Mystic Garden.

A big *'No Vacancies'* sign was now firmly, but sadly, posted at the edge of Eden along with the relevant *God Security* in the form of a giant, sword-brandishing, fiery angel. *'No humans allowed ~ please move along now!'* And move along they did, into a world rampant with a recently unleashed mimetic contagion. The desire genie was now well and truly out of the lamp of innocence. The primeval breaking news quizzically posed the question of the day, *'Who'll put him back?'*

So why did our Adamic ancestors have to pack up and leave the idyllic Eden? Is the Divine some kind of jealous despot who can't live with a bit of friendly competition? I believe the answer to that troubling question to be a resounding *'No'*. By definition, Divine Source can't be a competitive, rivalrous deity; all things constantly flow and return to Him as Sacred Unity. There has to be another reason for the unfortunate Adamic expulsion.

The sending away of the newly knowledgeable *couple was, for Divine Love, a painful, yet necessary act.* Humanity's original psychic wiring, created for imitative desire with Divine Love, had been short circuited by the viral desire for knowledge, the consciousness of *good and evil* i.e. morality. Morality, in its religious and humanistic guises has held mankind in its guilt induced grip ever since.

Before progressing further let me explain a little more about *mimetic or imitative desire,* a concept expounded in the works of French academic, *Rene Girard*. Simply put, Girard suggests that we humans catch or absorb our desires from others. He believes that we live in a great desire network or matrix in which we imbibe the desires of significant models before transmitting them on to some poor unsuspecting other; a rampant desire plague, without any apparent antidote.

The uncomfortable truth is that we humans aren't in control of our personal psyches as much as we imagine.

Unknown to us, the deadly *desire flow* repeatedly infects our unconscious, whilst our conscious *free will* mistakenly celebrates its hallucinatory autonomy.

What an insidious enemy our mutated, skewed desire really is; we aren't even aware of the insidious control it exercises over us. It's what makes the mass media world of advertising such a lucrative industry. Transmit a few subliminal desires via David Beckham and hey presto – watch the big bucks role in. The Edenic Serpent, whoever or whatever it represents, is clever for sure, a real marketing man at heart. Desire gravitates us towards our model-rivals like moons to their mother planet; thus the relentless path of psychological or material acquisition is established.

Perhaps George Lucas' Zen-like, Yoda, should have proclaimed *'The* **mimetic force** *is strong within you, young Skywalker!'* Model-rivals need only tug our desire chains in order to realign us with their own skewed desire. Girard calls such a mimetic system *the Satan*, or *Adversary* as it usually provokes confrontation, fractured relationships and ultimately scapegoating violence.

It's surely no coincidence that whenever Yeshua talks of Satan within the Gospel narratives it is always within a desire context. His desert confrontation, following His baptismal revelation of Divine Love, was with the three-fold desire for survival, fame and power. Unlike we dysfunctional sons of Adam, the Nazarene somehow overcame them all, though not by religious stoicism or pumped up will power, but through a harmonious mimetic alignment with the Divine Father. *'I only do the works that I see the Father do.'*

The Judean desert was momentarily transformed into a restored Eden for this *Second Adam*. This time around the angelic, Security team didn't ask the Yeshua Adam to leave, instead ministering to Him as the representative of a *New Mankind*. An archetypal Man once again in tune with the Divine desire for communion and oneness.

Where does this leave us 21st century Yeshua followers? Well, the rewiring of desire that was modelled in Yeshua is now available to us through Spirit. Our inner desire sensors have been realigned and reignited. It's now natural for one *born from above* to desire the Divine desires. This Spirit intervention well and truly puts religious asceticism and legalism in their proper place; no longer needed, thank you very much. Such is the essence of the Good News declared by the Nazarene.

'But, *but, but....*' we reflexively retort while struggling with the years of doctrinal programming (sorry teaching) that we've experienced at the hands of zealous preachers. *'My flesh, my flesh'* we painfully cry looking for a way out of our torturous desire prison. Paul/Saul of Tarsus, having been heavily into religion himself, both saw and understood this inner turmoil.

Instead of his term *flesh* let's substitute it with *skewed mimetic desire.* Like a recently renovated house we've been lovingly rewired by Spirit. Yes, the old wiring circuit remains but thankfully it's now unattached to our restored power supply.

On *awakening* to what Spirit has done we now automatically absorb our desire and power from the Divine supply. If we nod off again, back into *unawareness*, we can still be fooled by the old mimetic wiring. This movement back and forth between the mutually exclusive desire systems continues until we lie exhausted, finally surrendering to the finished work of the Master Electrician.

So why the 'Go Man Go' of this chapter's title? Throughout the scriptural narratives of all religions seekers after God were regularly asked to go here and go there by the Divine Voice. Why? Simply to avoid *mimetic desire.*

Abram, the founder of Judaism, was asked by his inner Voice to leave Ur of the Chaldees. Taking his old dad Terra with him, he courageously packed up before departing the safe familiarity of the city. Unfortunately however, the embryonic hero of faith stopped at the Assyrian city of Haran instead of pushing on into the fertile land of Canaan. Why? Mimetic desire. Terra, like all fathers, had a great mimetic pull over his adventurer son. The imitative desire flowed along the long established father - son axis. The result – Abram pitched camp in downtown Haran.

As we trace similar stories throughout the world's

sacred narratives, the Divine appears to require the seeker to geographically relocate in order to break their previously strong mimetic ties. Distance definitely helps. To respond to the Divine Voice is to forego mimetic desire posing as *loyalty* or *fear of the unknown*. When the Divine says go, always go.

A *going* always precedes a *growth* in spiritual awareness, due to its severance of the old mimetic pathways. Geography can influence one's level of psycho-spiritual maturity; amazing, but true. Beware of those around you with a strong desire pull; those who turn up the gravity notch imprisoning you in their own incestuous web.

So today, if Spirit is saying 'Go', don't think twice about it. Break free from your present mimetic network and respond to that still, small Voice. You won't regret it.

20

Mimetic Desire & Human Lids

As previously stated, I believe mimetic desire and its effects to be the nuts and bolts of what religious writings refer to as *sin*; a destructive dysfunction that afflicts mankind, breaking our experiential harmony with the Divine. Personally speaking, I now hate the almost meaningless 's' word; a religious term overlaid with so much sacred prejudice and misconceptions that it sends the average, open-hearted seeker running for cover.

Until Yeshua stepped into human history the malignant force of skewed mimetic desire worked away hideously behind the scenes, disguised as sacrificial religion, culture, ritual and indeed law. Please let me explain.

The tragic endgame of all imitative desire is communal violence that, if left unchecked, can run rampant, destroying the very fabric of a community. Mankind, in his flawed ingenuity, has created sacrificial religion to restrain such a violent flood. Rather than opting for a contagion of rivalry, our ancestors subliminally but insidiously selected an arbitrary individual as the cause of all the community's ills. This cleverly resulted in only *one* unfortunate group member permanently *checking out* thus saving the whole community from self-inflicted slaughter. I guess the poor, unfortunate guy or gal with six fingers, twisted limbs or bad body odour got the vital but deadly and deeply unenviable once in a lifetime opportunity.

Once the community had released its channelled violence onto Mr/Mrs victim, the mimetic rivalry's intense energy levels suddenly dissipated, falling back to a perverse level of equilibrium How smug the inventors of such a substitutionary system must have felt; at least until the irresistible virus of mimetic desire started its dastardly infection all over again.

"New victim wanted - no need to apply - we'll find you!"

Such *malicious* adverts were repeatedly posted all over the communal psyche; and find him/her they did. The tragic history of mankind is unfortunately full of dead but successful candidates.

As time progressed, the strong sense of community *peace* that followed such regular deaths and their newly associated ritual, began to be attributed to the favor of *the gods*.

"Oh I get it - if we're suffering communal problems then the gods must be angry. So we dispatch a suitable victim in their direction and hey presto, the placated gods smile on us again!"

Indeed, in some ancient societies the community

establishment decided that such was the level of cathartic peace following a termination that the victim themself must surely be a god.

"We sure have done the divine one a favour, sending them back to the spirit world so promptly. That's why they are blessing us so much from above. Oh the transcendent peace!"

The birth of *fallen* religious belief and ritual had now seemingly come to mankind's rescue. As human history progressed the unfortunate human victims were replaced by farm produce, doves, little cuddly lambs and all sorts of other goodies but, ingeniously, the dark mimetic mechanism remained the same. May I be blunt. Human culture, in which we take such pride, evolved around a violent act - the death or ostracism of the weak for the sake of community strength.

Thus, through sacrificial religion, ritual (the symbolic enactment of the communal blood lust) and law (a later, seemingly more *moral* development), human culture kept a lid on the explosive energies of imitative desire and its resulting violence. Escape valves were one thing but a root and branch solution was desperately needed.

Into such a desire bound world stepped the Nazarene prophet, Yeshua bar Yosef. How would the human community handle Him and His Aramaic message of *"malkutah alahah - the kingdom/queendom of God"*?

21

What's So Special About Yeshua?

Yeshua, the Nazarene prophet-teacher, has influenced human history more than any other man or woman since time immemorial. Apparently He didn't write a book, live in a palace, nor travel outside his national boundaries and yet became the central figure in world history under the Greek name: Jesus Christ. The image of his barbaric execution on a run of the mill Roman scaffold is the icon to surpass all icons.

What was He all about and what, perhaps more importantly, was the reason for His death? Was He God or man or both? If God, in what way was He God and why? Christian orthodoxy has formed belief systems over the millennia to place the Galilean Yeshua in His Jesus box as the dying Saviour of the world. In what way is He a Saviour and, perhaps more poignantly, can millions of Christians be wrong?

Let's start at the world of Yeshua's time. An era of tight religious and political control with human mimetic desire repressed by Jewish religious law and brutal Roman military force. Reformist Jewish movements provided their own particular take on national liberation for the now confused and largely disillusioned inhabitants of Galilee and Judaea. Some sought a hands on military strategy to evict the pagan Roman occupiers while others fanatically awaited the apocalyptic Kingdom of God in their purity obsessed ascetic desert communities. Into such a complex and seething world was born Yeshua bar Yosef, destined, perhaps unknown to Himself, to become the greatest spiritual leader of all time.

The most significant event for Yeshua, prior to His active itinerant ministry, was His baptism by his preacher cousin John, in the mystically revered Jordan river. It proved to be the inspirational key for all that followed in the fledgling prophet's life.

"You are my Beloved Son in whom I am well pleased."

Had these same words been previously whispered to the archetypal man Adam by the Divine Voice in the idyllic surroundings of prehistorical Eden? I believe so.

Yeshua, the Second Adam, rose out of the waters fully aware that He was now in total mimetic or imitative harmony with Divine Presence. A new Man whose desire centre was perfectly aligned with the Divine will. An intimate communion of God and Man that reflected the original creation but yet a new and perhaps even greater creation. Yeshua clearly encountered a *born from above* experience, one that He would later discuss with the puzzled Pharisee, Nicodemus. A mystical experience that profoundly illustrated that of the first Adam as Holy Breath discovered its first ever human dwelling.

In light of His Jordan, Spirit encounter, Yeshua's message and mission take on a radical new meaning as we re-examine the Gospel narratives. A man in total imitative desire with the Divine delight is now the messenger of a new Kingdom, a new Garden of Eden.

Unsurprisingly, those surrounding the Nazarene are expecting an old style returning Kingdom steeped in the rivalry of religion (Yahweh is *our* God) and of nationalistic politics (New Davidic style monarchy). Yeshua, however, wasn't going to get sucked into such a mimetic game, one that set brother against brother. Rather, His radical message was one of a Spirit engineered realignment of the dysfunctional human desire mechanism; a reset towards His Loving and non rivalling God known affectionately as Abba. No wonder that His closest friends and family feared for His mental health.

Throughout his three-year journey mimetic desire lay in wait for Yeshua, sometimes in the most respectable of guises. His encounters with the professional clergy of His day were often subtle attempts by the adversarial mimetic system to make him one of their own; a rivalrous rabbi who'd reinforce the existing boundary lines separating the *righteous* and the *unrighteous*. True to form, Yeshua wouldn't play their competitive games, eventually resulting in His terminal scapegoating by the religious and political powers of His day.

In the Greek New Testament, the unusual word *scandalon* appears in the Gospel narratives, usually spoken by Yeshua Himself. It's variously translated as stumbling block or snare which tends to hide its relative frequency and, I believe, its true significance. Literally, a scandalon is something we trip over on our journey. *Rene Girard*, the French academic, believes this to be one of the most significant and illuminating words in the New Testament. In his well argued *mimetic theory*, Girard believes that the term, scandalon, often refers to a person, a model-obstacle who blocks one's spiritual journey through desire rivalry.

One of the most interesting scenarios where scandalon occurs is Yeshua's announcement regarding His decision to travel up to Jerusalem to face death. Simon Peter, his most passionate and vociferous disciple, reflexively retaliates by declaring such a course of action to be completely out of the question. Yeshua's response is instantaneous and, at the same time, deeply fascinating. Swinging around He strongly rebukes Peter with the totally unexpected words:

> "Get behind me Satan (adversary), you are a **scandalon** to me!"

What a seemingly shocking response to one of His closest disciple friends. What did Yeshua mean? This is what I believe was going on behind this well-known religious scene.

Three years previously the big fisherman had left all to follow Yeshua on His religious road trip. Clearly, Yeshua had mimetically drawn Peter into His own desire for the *Kingdom of God*. Peter, for all his character flaws, had, like all disciples, begun to model himself on His rabbi master, while still not fully understanding the true meaning of Kingdom. He still believed that the Yeshua entourage would end up ruling a politically and religiously restored, Roman-free Israel. Peter had arrived at a relational stage where his still skewed mimetic desire had, in his eyes, turned him into a close advisor, indeed, almost an equal partner with Yeshua.

Peter subconsciously reckoned that he'd endured enough discipleship spadework and was close to becoming a reflected desire model for Yeshua. The shocking announcement of Yeshua's plans to walk straight into his enemies hands, flushed out Peter's monstrous double rivalry with His Master. Hence Yeshua's blunt but accurate verbal response.

Unconsciously playing the mimetic game, Peter had unwittingly become adversarial in his devoted relationship to Yeshua. In that brief outburst he revealed himself as the embodiment of the adversarial mimetic system known as the Satan. Yeshua wasn't rebuking a disembodied third party; He was looking straight at Peter when he delivered the unexpected rebuke.

Peter had become, without realising it, a scandalon, a stumbling block, a model obstacle to Yeshua and His Abba's channelled desire. The disciple's subliminal desire for power was trying to hook his Master and reel Him in. Without fully realising it, the zealous Peter was attempting to block Yeshua's final mission; that of exposing skewed mimetic desire and its violent fruit by means of His unjust and very public death.

Yeshua's declaration that Peter thought like a man and not God was a revelation in itself. Peter still wasn't in mimesis with Divine Desire by means of his relationship with Yeshua. Rather, his skewed desire centre was still alive and kicking, despite having had three years exposure to the spiritual alignment of his rabbi, Yeshua.

As Yeshua finally entered Jerusalem, the ritualistic forces of mimetic desire were already stirring. Within the week the adoring festival goers had turned into the lynch mob that condemned their previously proclaimed Messiah. The Chief Priest Caiaphas declared the insightful one liner:

"Better for one to die than all." John 18:14

The scene was now set for an ancient religious ritual, the enactment of a sacrificial rite born out of hyper mimetic desire and its concluding violence. Even his previously loyal disciples were caught up in the scapegoating of the Man without desire. Through their fear and passivity they joined in the sacramental blood lust of the mob and its rulers.

Even when facing death the Galilean prophet refused to be drawn into mimetic rivalry with the Sanhedrin and His accusers. His desire was His Abba's desire and He wouldn't change its alignment, even to save His own skin. On the Friday of His execution it certainly looked like the old mimetic system had won again; that the Satan was still deeply entrenched within the world's religious and political systems.

The beloved object of Yeshua's desire seemed strangely quiet over that haunting weekend; until Sunday morning that is when Mary and the other disciples finally realised that the power of Divine mimesis extends beyond the grave. The Abba Creator responded to the Second Adam by clothing Him with a reconstituted resurrection body; a Cosmic validation that shocked the dysfunctional principalities and powers of mankind's mimetic system. Divine Source had declared His hand by instituting a mimetic flow with the scapegoat victim of human culture rather than the cultural mechanisms that promised peace and stability; the powers that claimed Him as benefactor of their warped system.

Things could never be the same again. The Kingdom had unexpectedly come crashing in by the back door; mankind could once again return to The Garden. The Divine whisper, *'You are my Beloved in whom I am well pleased'*, would once more reach the psychic ear of the Adamic family.

Dylan Morrison

And what of the Nazarene?

A resurrected man, living outside space-time, in harmony once more with the Divine Delight; Yeshua Bar Alaha, Yeshua Son of God, the *Second Adam*.

Way Beyond The Blue

22

Why Do I Feel Weird In Church?

In this chapter I will attempt to make mimetic theory practical by helping the reader to identify the strange feeling that eventually creeps up on us after having regularly attended a church or alternative faith community. The pastor, minister, priest, rabbi or mullah has probably never enlightened you as to what it is, but it's there nonetheless, itching away under your devoted religious skin.

We've previously explored how Yeshua died to publicly expose and nullify *skewed mimetic* or *imitative desire*. Once this hidden control system is revealed for what it is, Yeshua, through Holy Breath, can realign us experientially into a direct harmony with the desire or Will of the Divine Father.

It reminds me of an experiment that we once performed in Physics class when I was knee-high to an Irish grasshopper and had lots of auburn hair. The class were given a piece of iron and told how its molecules were chaotic in nature, pointing in a multitude of directions. The magnets were then distributed to us and the instruction given to use them to stroke the iron in a particular direction.

Amazingly, after quite a few strokes our little pieces of iron absorbed the magnetic field of the magnet as its molecules came into harmony all pointing in the same direction. What a great little illustration of the power of mimesis. By drawing alongside us Spirit has brought our wayward and skewed desires into line with Divine delight.

Well that's the theory, but of course we're still living in the midst of a mimetic culture with its own particular gravitational field. Even as followers of Yeshua we tend to hop in and out of desire fields, viz. the Kingdom of God and our mimetic world system. The latter proudly boasts:

*"I want what you desire; indeed I want your desire, so that I can **be** you."*

Such is the world of psychic vampires that we inhabit. Daily, desire is drawn like blood during our relational encounters in the dark and hidden world of mimesis.

The collective of Yeshua followers, commonly known as the Church, has been given the task of modelling a community of Divinely restored mimetic desire. However, just because we're part of such a faith community doesn't guarantee that we're enjoying the freedom from skewed desire that Yeshua has initiated us into by Spirit.

So what is this strange feeling that I referred to earlier; the one that insists that something isn't quite right in your church? Instead of trying to backtrack to the source of such a feeling many of us jump on, what I mischievously call, the religious treadmill, in an effort to really fit in. Unfortunately, such a reaction results in things only getting worse as we spin our way to emotional and spiritual exhaustion.

The root problem is, however, quite easily identified. We have stepped out of imitative desire with Holy Breath, becoming a slave to the surrounding group mimesis. Sadly such a skewed desire matrix is what holds many religious groups together and indeed, gives them their own particular identity. Yeshua is honoured as the notional figurehead but more often than not the real mimetic centre of the community is the zealous pastor, minister or priest.

Scripture is often cleverly misinterpreted in order to keep the intense desire-show on the road. Adherents are unconsciously infected by the leader's apparent desire for God, leading to a gradual, subconscious attempt at imitating him/her. In my own bizarre experience, even my handwriting style became a clone of that of my pastor. Yes, I had it bad, but that's another story as detailed in my memoirs.

Unfortunately such a leader-centred desire matrix must eventually lead to intense competition and rivalry surprisingly disguised as commitment to the pastor, community or even God Himself. Such rivalry eventually leads to departures and splits as the faith leader begins to sense the ever nearing approach of their desire clones. Like bible toting zombies of the night, such devotees are usually frozen out of community life by their model man/woman of God by means of tighter control or emotional expulsion.

*"If you've become like me then you might **replace** me!"*

On rare occasions the model leader is the one who must depart due to the dependency addiction of his disciple clones. Nervous breakdowns, illicit affairs with their accompanying marital problems are usually the results of an intense desire matrix apexed in the professional faith leadership.

So, if you regularly left church feeling worse than when you went in, stop and ponder. Your skewed desire alarm has probably been activated deep within your psyche. You've probably just sat through a dysfunctional exchange of desire that has blocked your new-found mimetic harmony with Divine Spirit. Shocking but true.

Why not spread the word around about this wolf in sheep's clothing? If you do, we Yeshua's followers might start enjoying the Divine life flow that He promised to all and sundry.

23

Dysfunctional Religious Attachments

Recovering from abuse experienced within a religious setting is a long and often painful process. While the level of abuse can vary along a given spectrum there are some observable characteristics common to all cases.

In the same way that alcoholics deny their drink problem or a battered spouse their partner's violence, so too the victims of religious abuse. Deep within the victim's psyche exists a gnawing feeling that something isn't just quite right. Yet a strong emotional attachment still locks the victim, for that's what they truly are, into a desire-control matrix. The first step to freedom is to admit that one may be imprisoned in such a dysfunctional system.

I would like to identify a number of phenomena linked to subliminal control that might clarify whether or not you're undergoing a level of religious abuse.

The elevation of your group above all other faith groups.

A clear danger sign is the exclusive nature of such religious groups. The *'God has chosen us to be special'* syndrome is a revealing symptom of a prevalent control mentality.

Broken or distrustful relationships with previous friends or family.

A *them and us* mental stronghold leads to emotional fractures with those previously close to the victim. When my wife and I finally left our Shepherding group, a highly educated elder's wife asked the pastor in a church meeting whether or not it was advisable to discuss *family business* with us if she accidentally met us in town. Thankfully, and, frankly to my great surprise, she was encouraged to be as open as she wished to be. Yet the fact that such a question was asked at all revealed a level of mistrust that was prevalent between those who remained and those who moved on.

A level of **commitment** *to the group that eats up time, money and emotional energy that's often to the detriment of normal family life.*

Often a commitment to God is interpreted as a commitment to the group. In my opinion this is a clear sign of near cultic tendencies within a faith body.

A strong charismatic leader with an elevated view of his own position and service.

The enthusiastic and deeply sincere believer can be drawn

to the charisma of their leader by means of mimetic or imitative desire; one longs to be as close to God as he/she appears to be. Such *followers* can, without realising it, greatly inflate a leader's view of his/her own importance, resulting in further religious delusion and its accompanying control.

A one-man-band leader who insists on fulfilling all the public service of the faith group.

Variety is a strong characteristic of Divine creation and should be reflected in the life of an organic faith community. It's not just the 'Rev. John Doe's Show'.

A casual dismissal of genuine concerns by the leader or leadership.'We know best, that's why God has made us leaders.'

If the leadership team of your faith group is regularly ignoring or belittling your and others' feelings of unease then it usually suggests an attitude of superiority within the team's membership.

"God's appointed us to leadership and there we'll always remain; we interpret any disagreement with us as a lack of 'faith' on your part".

Some religious leaders utilise a standard psychological technique whereby, on leaving private meetings with them, the follower has the false impression that the problem they'd just aired was their fault all along; the religious status quo thus maintaining itself yet again. Such a sacred mind game is most effective in keeping all honest dissenters at bay.

A secrecy regarding the financial expenditure of the group, especially regarding the leader's salary.

Many faith groups have a well tested technique for concealing details of financial expenditure. The salaries of all employed workers are grouped together at the AGM giving the impression of an equality within the group's salary structure. The opposite is often the case. If your group is secretive about detailed expenditure, asking you to trust them, then beware. You may well be under a form of financial control that is contrary to basic honesty and integrity.

A regular feeling of guilt regarding your 'service' to God via the group.

Guilt has nothing to do with being a follower of Yeshua. If service guilt lands on you while attending a faith group then you are being abused. The Divine never uses guilt to motivate His children.

*A special **in** language that outsiders can't understand.*
An apparently innocent language is used within the group

that reinforces the hidden agenda of the abusive system. In my own case such phrases as *'being under authority'* and *'covering'* were incorrectly revered as terms of spiritual correctness.

A lack of vulnerability on behalf of the main leader or teacher.

Most abusive leaders are locked into denial regarding their own flaws and weaknesses, often appearing stronger to their followers than they really are. Yet ironically a level of vulnerability and openness is often required in followers by such a leader in his counselling role. Such a one-way openness inadvertently channels the follower into a deeper infantile mindset, thus maintaining the abusive matrix. Remember, *knowledge is power* within the pastoral world of an abusive faith group.

In the next chapter I'll suggest some effective ways of freeing oneself from the subtlety of such spiritually destructive control.

Dylan Morrison

24

Inner Space 1 ~ To Boldly Go Where No Preacher's Gone Before

The search for meaning and our place in the cosmos continues at a frantic pace. Scientists are exploring two seemingly paradoxical aspects of our material universe; the mysterious distant edges of outer space and the sub-atomic world of photons where quantum theory appears to rule as king. Our fascination with *out there* and *inside this* has increased dramatically with the development of new technologies that let us examine these two mysterious worlds.

As in the material, or apparent material realm, so in the spiritual realm. Man has always been fascinated by the transcendence of God, his *out there-ness and His immanence, the within-ness of Spirit*. One thing we can be sure of is that God, by definition, must be everywhere or omnipresent, while intimately dwelling within each of us in a way we don't fully understand.

What or who are we, these tabernacle-tents of the Divine? That's the $64,000 question we face during our mysterious Earthly sojourn. *Anthony de Mello*, the inspiring Catholic mystic whose writings were banned by *Pope Benedict* in his previous incarnation as *Cardinal Ratzsinger*, has something profound to say:

> "The big question for us is not "Who is God?" or "Who is Jesus Christ?" but **"Who am I?"**."

Many have given up the traditional religious quest to focus on this important and deeply disturbing question. Mind, Body, Spirit gurus of all hues send us in the direction of *Self-Realisation* in order to discover the meaning of existence. Christians and various other religiously attached believers immediately dismiss this whole approach as narcissistic nonsense. *So who's right?*

As a follower of Yeshua, the Nazarene, I love His summary of our life purpose in two simple, but yet profound, statements:

> "Love the Lord your God with all your heart, soul, mind and strength."

> "Love your neighbour as your**self**."

On my own tortuous journey I've seen many sincere folk who claim to do both, but the overwhelming evidence would appear to suggest otherwise. Certainly many of us are convinced of our love for God as evidenced by our lemming-like attachment to various religious programmes. Like little hamster disciples, we run the wheel of self-denial in order to convince the Divine of our unquestionable devotion. Thankfully, the secret of loving God, is paradoxically to let Him passionately Love us with the embrace of Presence; a communion for the hidden place, rather than the public religious marketplace known as church. Only then will we be ready to return His Love in both His and our neighbours direction.

However, the real trouble begins here; many of us can't love our neighbours as we don't yet love ourselves. In fact, we don't even know who or what our *Self* is. Our conscious sense of identity is often a clever forgery, produced by a deep, inner, gnawing pain. A false identity to help us survive the primal wounding of our childhood and the traumatic pains of later life.

When the religious convert has a sudden, dramatic encounter with Divine Spirit he is never the same again. A channel has been opened through which Divine Love and Presence may now flow freely, but still there remains much pain in the darkest reaches of his/her psyche that cries out for attention; the attention known as healing.

Life is a river of healing; a journey into a wholeness that the Divine means us to enjoy, yet, such a process takes time, not just the instant fix of a one-off encounter with Spirit. This is where many Charismatics and Pentecostals Yeshua followers are misinformed. Divine reconstruction is an encounter followed by a lifetime of healing; how else can one explain so many broken marriages and secret addictions among the leaders of such groups?

False identities or egos abound within such communities. I should know, for I used to have one or two of my own in my Charismatic incarnation. At the opposite end of the religious spectrum, conservative doctrine-obsessed believers rarely get out of their heads, leaving their psychic wounding to fester like an old sore in the unacknowledged basement of their lives. Out of sight, out of mind seems to be the approach taken here.

"Smile, Jesus loves you. Just keep reading your Bible!"

*"Yes I know, but do you love your **Self**?"*

Let's be honest, most of us who claim to know God are as emotionally screwed up as the next guy. It's just not acceptable to talk about such issues as we might let the Almighty down. A declaration of psychic weakness might prove to be negative PR for the Divine cause and the institutions who push an ethereal salvation.

In the next few chapters I will investigate further the inner healing journey; a journey suggested by Italian psychologist, *Roberto Assagioli*. One of the few 20th century psychologists to acknowledge the existence of Divine Spirit, Assagioli's model is, to my mind, a perfect fit for the mysticism of Yeshua.

A poignant little story that reveals Assagioli's genuine humility and spirituality goes something like this:

During World War 2, Mussolini and his Italian

Fascists got extremely worried about Assagioli, his psychological theories and his disinterest in the Italian master race. Like all good dictators, Mussolini had the psychologist imprisoned, placing him in solitary confinement. A few months later a leaner and thinner Assagioli was released and to the amazement of his captors thanked them for his time alone. When asked why he responded by claiming that he'd used the golden opportunity to get in touch with the Divine and had encountered a joy like none other before.

I don't know about you, but that sounds like my kind of guy. Let's have a look at what he has to say about our spiritual and emotional condition in the next chapter.

25

Inner Space 2 ~ The Egg & Our Inner World

In the previous chapter, I suggested that we have a look at Roberto Assagioli's model of the psyche, in order to apply its findings to our search for *Self*-understanding. Assagioli, a one time disciple of the renowned Carl Jung, was probably the most genuinely humble of the 20th century's Psychology pioneers. That's why you've probably never heard of him; unlike Dr Freud and his former mentor, Dr Jung, Roberto wasn't heavily into PR.

Assagioli claimed a number of spiritual experiences during his early life which motivated him to develop his famous Egg model of the psyche; a much needed attempt to synthesise the seemingly disparate worlds of spirituality and psychology. Like all psycho-spiritual models it's just that, a model of the inner Self, so please don't initially reject it with a barrage of Scripture texts or philosophical jargon. I've recently found it extremely helpful on my journey of discovery; I believe you will too.

Assagioli proposed that our psyche can be likened to an *egg* split horizontally into three levels; the *higher unconscious*, the *middle unconscious*, and the *lower unconscious*. So far so good, a healthy individual being described as one who can welcome and incorporate each of these psychological levels into their sense of identity or I. The Italian psychologist saw these three levels as a product of a number of traumatic splits during early childhood. In other words, as the child's embryonic sense of Self was forming, a lack of empathetic mirroring by caregivers caused the developing psyche to take emergency action and split itself into three.

The cumulative pain of such a sense of non-being is, Assagioli suggests, stored in the dark basement of the lower unconscious. It's the place where the results of separation and its accompanying existential angst are stored, like a pile of psychological dirty linen, lying undiscovered by the survival seeking conscious mind.

Although seemingly hidden and securely locked away, these traumatic memories and their resulting psychic disease influence much of who we are in adulthood. In light of my own experiences, I'd humbly suggest that conversion to a religious or spiritual world view doesn't, in itself, guarantee the unlocking of this repressed cellar nor, perhaps more importantly, the admittance of Divine Light into the dark recesses of our skeletal cupboard. But more of this lower unconscious in future chapters.

Most of us appear to spend our daily lives within the realm of the middle unconscious, a fairly friendly terrain where we camp in a little secure tent called *consciousness*, our field of *knowing*. This middle unconscious may be likened to a giant filing cabinet, from which consciousness can pull out required data at a moments notice.

"Now where did I put my keys?"

Free access to such information is usually granted by the middle unconscious as our really traumatic information is safely locked away in the storeroom of the lower unconscious. It is here, within the realm of our consciousness, that a fragile sense of *I* or *Me* exists. It's a pale shadow of who we really are, being mainly based on the safe material to hand in our middle unconscious.

Assagioli suggested that we also possess the higher unconscious, a realm that in many ways is also still under lock and key. This is the realm of our intuition and its often unexplainable experiences. It's also the apparent channel for the *Other* or *Spirit* of religious parlance; the doorway to alternative states of consciousness and unitive spiritual encounters. Largely sidelined by the ruling consciousness it too is explained away as pure brain function by the sceptical community referred to as neuroscientists. Such a higher unconscious is the residency for significant dreams, gut feeling and ultimately the border crossing for Divine Presence.

Assagioli imagined this egg shaped model of the human psyche as suspended within the ocean of, what he referred to as, *The Transpersonal Self*; the ultimate reality behind and within all things. Interestingly, such a Transpersonal Self, was even perceived to permeate the three levels of the human psyche; a pickled egg of sorts, floating in the Divine Ocean.

Within these levels of the unconscious live the internal actors of our life drama; the survival based sub-personalities, each trying to hog the limelight in our own unique personality theatre. Most of us won't or can't acknowledge their underground existence although I suspect that those close to us are all too painfully aware of their little performances. More of them later.

What are the applications and consequences of Assagioli's model for those desiring to receive Divine Love and give it away to a broken, dysfunctional humanity?

We'll have a look at those pressing issues in the next chapter.

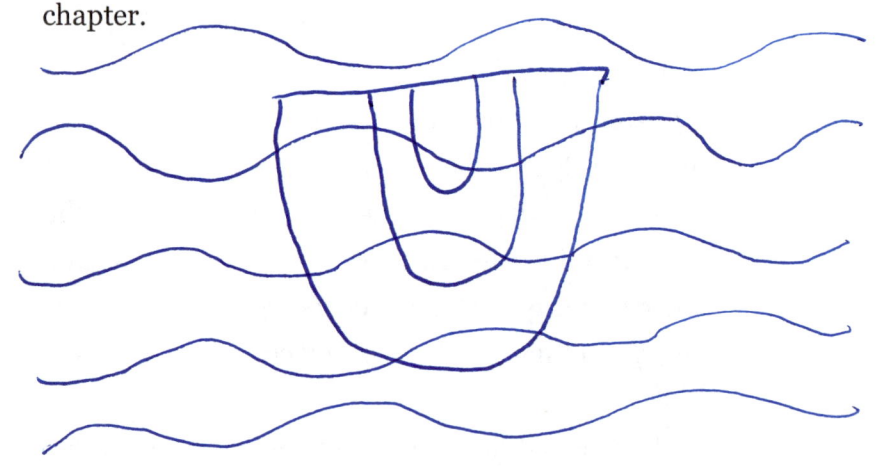

26

Inner Space 3 ~ Sacred Unity

In the previous chapter, I introduced Roberto Assagioli's three layered *egg model* of the human psyche and its possible application to our spiritual journey. In this chapter I intend to explore how important *integration* is to both our mental and spiritual health.

According to the traditional Gospel accounts, Yeshua appeared to be the sort of guy who lived life out of a deep inner peace, believing Himself to be at One with his *Abba* God. Such a belief birthed the Nazarene's claim to only do what He saw the Divine Father do, especially with regard to His numerous acts of physical and emotional healing.

Statements like this have been the theological bedrock for the case of Yeshua's divinity from which the philosophical concept of *The Trinity* later evolved. However, I'm presently more interested in whether we, as followers of Yeshua, can, as He claimed, enjoy the same sort of Oneness with the Divine that He enjoyed and, if so, how it can be practically experienced in our daily lives.

In Aramaic, the day to day language spoken by Yeshua, the word for God is *Alaha*. Each time we read of Yeshua referring to God in the Gospel narratives it's Alaha that He uses to denote the Divine. Today, both Christians of the Egyptian Coptic Church and followers of Islam use the word *Allah*, an Arabic derivative of the Aramaic Alaha, to describe their own particular Divinity. Unknown to many, the root meanings of both words are *sacred unity*, *Oneness* and *the One without an opposite.* In other words, Yeshua referred to God and by implication Himself as a Oneness or Spirit Unity.

If, as the author of Genesis claims, we were originally created in the image of God then surely we too can expect to experience a spiritual and psychological Oneness when restored to life as it was originally intended. Rather than embed us more and more deeply into the Greek based dualistic *them and us* mindset, a genuine encounter with Holy Breath or Spirit releases us into a state of consciousness that enhances our inherent Oneness.

Here is where I believe Assagioli's *egg' model* can prove useful as we explore further the Divine nature as reflected by Yeshua. May I daringly suggest that many followers of the great monotheistic faiths neither perceive nor indeed experience this inner unity having been locked into a titanic struggle of *good versus evil* both within and without. Assagioli suggested that when one's *I* begins to glimpse the unseen elements of the unconscious realm, then one has started on the path to inner *integration* or *unity;* a conformity to the Divine image as promised and reflected by Yeshua Himself.

However, we must face up to a serious hurdle before tackling such an inner integration. Our unconscious areas are populated by little clusters of survival personalities that have secretly held us together for many years. These *sub-personalities* are terrified of such an integration, fearing annihilation, the illusory end game of the fractured human psyche. Let's take a look at a few simple examples of these hidden, psychic rescuers.

Early on in life, a little girl learns to be a *Tom boy* in order to obtain her father's approval. Perhaps she's surrounded by sporting brothers who easily connect with their deeply competitive father. What is she to do but birth a new male persona, through which to win the conditional love of the most important man in her life. Fast forward many years, and the now mature woman is hitting problems in her relationships with men. Repressed femininity and a *one of the lads* mentality rides to the rescue as soon as sexual intimacy threatens to encroach upon the wounded soul.

A happily married successful business man appears to be the epitome of self confidence. Yet, on visiting his elderly mother, his wife observes him undergo a complete change in character. A little lost boy persona, transforms him into a compliant slave to his mother's unrealistic demands. Roll back the years, to a fierce encounter for the four year old boy. Having accidentally spilt a pot of paint on an expensive carpet, the lad is severely beaten as a frustrated mother shouts, *'What did I tell you?'* Locked away in the darkness of the basement, a new sub-personality emerges. One that vows never to displease *mother* again.

The sub-personality realm within carries a unique range of potential permutations, one reflecting our own particular childhood traumas. How then is our spiritual journey to proceed? The answer lies in further understanding as to how these splits in our psyche emerged. It's really quite shockingly simple; a lack of adequate parental empathy and Self-reflection results in a paralysing fear of non-being, triggering the formation of such sub-personalities. A fragmentation of the developing Self that accompanies us into the seemingly dangerous life ahead.

Identifying and then *welcoming* these independently competing entities into the family of our unified Self is the key to psychological and spiritual wholeness. The easiest way to understand such a healing process, is to imagine the human psyche as a stage where a diversity of performing players are welcomed and appreciated. Our sub-personalities have performed backstage for many, many years, usually in the darkness of our lower unconscious. There they've competitively bickered over the leading role of Self saviour, resulting in a constant state of divisive emotional angst, much to the embarrassment of our spirit

'I' sitting patiently in the stalls. Together, such sub-personalities comprise our <u>overall survival personality</u>, one that must be welcomed and embraced for its important but deeply inadequate role in protecting us from the pain of our formative primal wounding. All cast members must now be invited onto the public stage, brought out into the open if you like, to participate in the conscious drama that is our psychological and spiritual life.

Rather than hog the backstage positions as before, each sub-personality now has its allotted role to play in the new *born again* production, under the directorship of the recently appointed *spirit I* and its determined assistant producer *human will*. The previously hidden, mini personalities, now perform at a *legitimate* time and place, adding to the rich texture of our lives and enabling us to truly be at peace with ourselves, perhaps for the first time ever.

A trained spiritual counsellor or therapist may be able to assist us in this critical stage of our development, acting as an empathic validation centre by providing a safe environment for such debuts on the stage of our consciousness. How traditional religious teaching may block such a healing process, and why many followers of Yeshua cling desperately onto the lifeboat of rational consciousness will be the topic of my next chapter.

27

Inner Space 4 ~ Fake Faith

In the previous chapter I considered the Middle Eastern idea of God as *Sacred Unity* and how such a natured Divinity works patiently towards the reintegration of all things. A God of Oneness cannot, by definition, settle for anything less. Perhaps, from the Divine viewpoint outside space-time, that reintegration has *always* been. Is it only our linear, time-based consciousness that perceives the world as a broken, fragmented place crying out for healing and restoration.

Our survival personality or ego loves the competitive nature of such fragmentation, continually jousting for the supposedly safe position of top dog, as it plays its rivalrous and often dangerous game. The wounded Self refuses to take heed of the recurring Divine message:

> "You can never be healed of your deep pain through victory over the other; the deadly spiral of rivalry and competition takes you further down into the realm of your primal wounding, the lower unconscious, the home of your fragmented sub-personalities."

Do we faith-filled-folk also live through our survival selves? I believe so. Doesn't faith release us from the tyrannical grip of our split psyche with all its clamouring voices? Well, I guess it all depends on our definition of faith. If faith is just a nod of the head to a bunch of religious beliefs, then it doesn't help one bit. While the conscious mind may receive a measure of peace and satisfaction from holding such theological concepts, the hidden sub-personalities still merrily control the human psyche from the darkness of the lower Self.

In my own religious incarnation I believed all the 'right things' *about* God yet remained deeply fragmented at a psychic level. Unfortunately the consensus of religious thought doesn't help us here, for we're instructed to hold onto the *facts* of our faith and strongly distrust our sensory feelings, the *'let me out'* cries of our repressed survival personalities.

I've met very few believers over the years who don't suffer from this inner struggle and its accompanying psychic pain. In fact, I'd humbly suggest that's the reason why some believers eventually chuck it all in, returning to a more hedonistic lifestyle, hoping to dull their inner angst. One of the inherent problems with traditional religious belief is that it has viewed this inner battle as a conflict between *Spirit* and *Satan*, the much hated Nemesis of God.

The cries for attention and acknowledgement that emanate from our inner sub-personalities are interpreted as the voice of a disruptive *Adversary*, who continually disturbs the inner peace of the believer. Such a dualistic belief institutionalizes our internal struggle, one from which we zealous souls are strangely loath to quit. Indeed to quit such a fight is judged to be a great act of betrayal; a dastardly act of surrender to demonic foes on the infamously one-way road to hell.

May I suggest that this false overlay, so easily placed on the fragile human psyche, is the reason for the underlying mistrust within religious circles of the unconscious areas in a believer's personality. *'Better not to go there'* is the seemingly wise advice given by highly suspicious and often ignorant pastoral advisors. Bible reading, more prayer and programmed church attendance are patronisingly offered to us as the only weapons fit to quell our inner turmoil, yet the psychic pressure within only intensifies. Our insidiously experienced sub-personalities only kick back more vigorously in response to such stoical efforts at religious asceticism.

To some more enlightened believers, faith is not only an intellectual assent to established dogma but also a deep *trust* in the God of their belief system. These dear souls appear to enjoy an inner harmony but unfortunately, all is not as it appears. While life throws them a blessing, their trust in the Divine soars high, but as soon as a curved ball is pitched in their direction they retreat into the well worn dualistic battle mode of the righteous warrior, with all his secret store of inner demons.

Struggles like this often end in illusory victories for the believer and his/her God, as the internal tensions are once more locked away by the seemingly victorious conscious mind. However, in my own experience, such victories are usually short-lived with the disguised unconscious voices and tensions returning once more to request validation from my spirit *I*. Most believers once more blame the Satan or Adversary, for such emotional turmoil and the inner battle re-intensifies. A *demonic* spiral indeed.

Facing such a predicament can we find any help in the teaching or practice of Yeshua, the perfectly integrated reflection of Sacred Unity? The Nazarene certainly seemed able to bring a sense of deep peace and acceptance to all those He encountered. Moral categories didn't seem to bother Him as he taught and manifested the unconditional Divine Love of His God, *Abba*.

The folk he'd real problems with were those religious leaders who peddled their dualistic world view of *the righteous* and *the sinners*. Their own internal dualism, firmly based on the security of Law observance, kept Yeshua's open offer of reconciliation and oneness at bay. Much modern religious thought still incorporates this highly dualistic modality. As a result, righteous believers are unknowingly imprisoned through a subliminal suppression of those aspects of their psyches, birthed by primal wounding.

Perhaps this is why the rejects of society were more receptive to Yeshua and his inclusive teaching on Divine Love. More often than not, the so-called sinners' sub-personalities ran rampant in full public display while those of the righteous lay deep within the religiously bolted prisons of their lower unconscious. As Yeshua ate and drank with society's rejects He was welcoming their broken, fragmented psyches into the wholeness of Divine Love. True healing indeed.

Much has been written about the exorcisms that Yeshua performed. The religious dualism of His day understood separate spiritual entities or demons to be rampant within society. Let's have a look at the demoniac known to his community and, indeed more importantly, to himself as *Legion*.

Clearly this was one fragmented guy, with inner turmoil beyond belief. His regular practice of self-mutilation and choice of a graveyard condominium were, to say the least, ominous. A man with psychic fragmentation to end all psychic fragmentation; a man deeply at war with him*self*. His nickname Legion would suggest that numerous traumas had birthed a multitude of psychic sub-personalities, split offs from his developing childhood I. The Gospel narratives seem to suggest such an I to have almost completely disappeared.

The demoniac's apparent chance meeting with Yeshua proved to be both dramatic and life changing. Divine energy, in the form of unconditional love, coursed through the Nazarene, bringing instant healing and the reintegration of the man's tortured psyche. No longer was there a need for such a massive internal personality split.

Yeshua cleverly allowed the demonic sub-personalities to have their individual *space-identity* in the local pigs, resulting in the reunified soul now sitting before Him, 'sane and in his right mind'. This demonstration of the dynamic power of Divine empathy disturbed the dualistic world view of the locals so much that they refused Yeshua entry to their nearby town. To the Gadarenes, the old dualistic paradigm of history was a much safer and conservative option than the Presence of Sacred Unity standing in their midst.

Today, I believe, many of us have fallen into the same trap; valuing our dissected dualism over psychic wholeness; tragically resulting in an intense inner and outer disintegration. In Yeshua's world view, barriers are a thing of the past, an aberration of the unified soul. May I suggest that, *genuine faith*, is a radical trust in the Oneness of all creation, the Oneness of our inner Selves and our eternal Union with Abba, the Source of all living things. With that in mind, let's give up the fake version.

28
Inner Space 5 ~ The Road To Wholeness

For fragmented humanity the road to wholeness or holiness is a long and often painful journey but one that's ultimately worth it. Life is the Divine opportunity for the reintegration of our fractured soul's many and varied facets. A few spiritual seekers run enthusiastically down this healing road but most of us chicken out by pitching camp in a nearby meadow until the day we're air-lifted out by death; a seemingly much easier option. What have we missed out on by carefully avoiding our pre-scripted healing journey? Why do we turn instead to the pain numbing effects of addictions for our much needed Soul relief?

I believe that by travelling such a wide yet destructive path we miss the opportunity to resonate with the Divine heartbeat for broken humanity. By definition, the Divine is a *healing* Presence, a unifier of our fractured cosmos and a restorer of a deeply divided mankind. Following the Way of healing is a true path of discovery; a discovery of Sacred Unity, the One from whom all things flow.

Yes, Wisdom is One, but she can interact with everyone else; she never needs to renovate, yet she doesn't hesitate to innovate, she influences one generation after another, turning them into friends of God and the prophets.

Wisdom 7:27

May I suggest, that Yeshua, the Galilean rabbi prophet, saw His own healing mission in such a light, viz. the reintegration of humanity to its Divine image; the return of a prodigal mankind to its Father's House, where a joyous reunion awaits. Indeed, so gripped was Yeshua by this focused sense of mission, that He willingly threw Himself into the darkest depths of splintered humanity by undergoing an unjust and barbarous religio-political execution.

The Nazarene's resulting resurrection experience heralded a reunified humanity whose traumatic split from Divine Source was lost in the illusory mists of time. The space-time epoch of separation was finally over; indeed, had it ever really existed within the Kingdom realm of Spirit? Oneness with Yeshua's, *Abba* God, was clearly revealed as the Alpha and Omega of Ultimate Reality. So how then do we experience this newly-won wholeness?

I believe that our transformation starts with a niggling dissatisfaction with our personal *status quo,* accompanied by a reactivated psychic hunger for growth and wholeness. Such tell tale signs are increasingly accompanied by a realisation that behind the seemingly fragmented inner and outer worlds of our conscious experience, lies a loving, welcoming, all-embracing Unity; the deeper, underlying Essence that we in the West commonly call God.

The road to psycho-spiritual growth that stretches out before us comprises the following two parallel tracks that we can travel along simultaneously:

The Transpersonal or Other Awareness track
&
The Self-Knowledge track

Many of us are further along one or other of these tracks, usually to the detriment of our progress on the other. To put it simply, some of us are *religious,* attempting the journey to Reality by following the traditional God signpost. Others pride themselves in having no time for *that sort of dogma thing*, following instead the signs pointing towards personal *Self development*. On this track the destination is a more *powerful* and possibly *successful* sense of I, usually residing within the realm of our middle unconscious.

Extreme examples of one-sided travellers may be monks or nuns (Transpersonal) in contrast to freshly confident, successful businessmen (Self-Knowledge). Each, having progressed along their particular specialist track, may be totally ignorant of the complementary healing process that awaits them on their parallel but relatively unexplored path.

The devout religious believer, who has genuinely experienced the Transpersonal may, incongruously, be a secret alcoholic or serial adulterer. Their painful path to healing tends take them through their repressed and multi-fractured psyche. Here the services of a wise and experienced therapist may be required. Their role as a *authentic unifying centre* can prove vital in providing a source of unconditional love during their surgical exploration of their patient's early primal wounding. Such believers don't require more zealous prayer/fasting/sermons but a fresh discovery of their own inner Self, perhaps for the first time in their earthly sojourn,

From my own observations, many religious groups sadly avoid recommending such a course of action for their *unhappy* followers. Such folk tend to eventually lose their particular take on *the faith* as their broken psyches desperately search for meaningful Self-expression outside the confines of their previous religious home.

The seemingly godless, secular, high achievers, on the other hand, may possess a most definite sense of Self, having a genuinely advanced knowledge of their inner strengths and weaknesses. In other words, they're aware of *what makes them tick.* These valuable lessons have often been painfully learnt through repeated failures within their social/business spheres. Failure is always a messenger sent by our inner Self, one desperately trying to get our complete and undivided attention.

However, some of these Self-Knowledge folk may also be operating out of a strong *survival* personality birthed by early primal wounding. In such cases, a *Transpersonal Crisis* often arrives unexpectedly, in order to free them from such an unbalanced view of Self; the resulting

> *In all created beings, O Lord, you find a spark of your own immortal spirit. Your imperishable spirit is in all things.* — Wisdom 12:1

Dylan Morrison

disintegration enabling them to see their own brokenness for, perhaps, the first time in their adult life. A so-called *mid-life crisis* often acts as a channel of communication for our desperate, downtrodden, authentic Self. It may also become the Voice through which the Transpersonal jolts us out of our slumber into a new spirit-awareness, and a welcome but unexpected place at the Divine table.

Like the two wings of a perfectly balanced bird in flight, *authentic Self knowledge* and *Spirit encounter* help us glide effortlessly toward our Life's joint goals; to be marinated in the Oneness of our Creator Source and to be One within. If we're feeling trapped by life maybe it's time to have a careful look at our second wing.

Holy Breath

Holier than thou
scapegoating
Survival/survival mode, what I have, what I provide
Smart NP
what others think about me
INNOCENT
work, what I DO
power & control
what I wear

Divine Spark
IMAGO DEI
Risen ONE

> *God did not make death, nor does He rejoice in the destruction of the living; For He fashioned all things that they might have being,* Wisdom 1:14
>
> *For God formed man to be imperishable; the image of His own nature He made him.* Wisdom 2:23

Way Beyond The Blue

Yeshua Sayings That You Rarely Hear In Church ~ 1

"The Son of Man came eating and drinking and they're saying "Look! A gluttonous human and tippler, tribute collectors' and sinners' friend"."

In this and the following three chapters I will examine four, relatively unknown yet New Testament sayings of Yeshua, the Galilean prophet whose forthright teaching challenged the civil and religious powers of His day.

If we presuppose that the Divine exists then He must surely be an *inclusive* God. A Being, responsible for the Cosmos and beyond, must love variety, welcoming it back into its original place in the Divine scheme. A Creator Source must, by reason of His very nature, embrace all that has been birthed by His Divine Will and Energy. Being responsible for it all, He must lovingly hold it close to His beating heart in all its multifarious totality.

Such was the view of Yeshua bar Yosef, the first-century, itinerant, Jewish preacher, who burst onto an expectant religious scene proclaiming the inclusive reign of God to his slightly sceptical, *seen it all before,* Galilean audiences. As with religious devotees throughout the ages, many of His early supporters eventually walked away, disillusioned by such an inclusive vision.

The common consensus required a Warrior King, steeped in the prevalent, dualistic, Jewish mindset, who'd get rid of the Roman occupation force *(them)* and restore Jewish independence to Yahweh's chosen people *(us)*. Steeped in Divine Wisdom, Yeshua wasn't going to join in such a divisive game.

Within the Middle Eastern social norms, hospitality and the sharing of meals with strangers was high on one's priority list. If you ate with someone you were making a profound relational statement. The trouble though was that not everyone got invited. The *us* and *them* mindset had undermined traditional Jewish hospitality in the guise of religious and political moral correctness. Society was deeply split into the never the twain shall meet groupings of *the righteous* and *the sinners.* Into such a segregated social scene stepped the Nazarene with His radical message of Divine inclusion.

As an itinerant preacher, Yeshua received numerous dinner invitations from His listeners. Sometimes, a call from a curious Pharisee to share a few hours theological discussion around a tasty meal. Sometimes a call from the local brothel, where the girls wanted to hear more about

His take on *Abba* God, through his mesmeric gift of storytelling. No matter who the host, Yeshua gladly accepted such opportunities to flesh out His Father's love.

However, in responding positively to the invitation of Jewish sex-workers and swindling government custom officials, Yeshua was also making a deeply provocative statement, one that can be summarised as follows:

> *I, and my Abba God, don't require moral change before accepting our so called sinner hosts as friends.*

Through their generous invitations the sinner class revealed a glimpse of their true spiritual condition; one of openness and honesty. That rare qualification proved to be enough for Yeshua and, He believed, for His God, as they sought to reconnect to a broken humanity.

Not surprisingly such a radical inclusion, outside the moral conformity of a skewed Torah observance, wasn't welcomed with open arms by His fellow God followers. The rule-keeping brigade were frankly distraught.

> *This just can't be right. Yahweh has given us the Torah to separate the sheep from the goats. Now this Galilean upstart is eating and drinking with the goats!*

The wonderfully insightful tale of Yeshua lodging for the night at Zaccheus' richly furnished apartment, backs up this radical new approach to religious *outcasts*. Amazingly, the vertically challenged Zac had no qualms about welcoming the Galilean rabbi into His hated family circle.

More amazing perhaps, is Yeshua's request to eat with the perceived traitor in the first place. As a top customs official, Zac would have milked the average Jew for as much as he could get, by fair means or, more commonly, foul. No wonder he was rich. Such an exemplary extortionist would have been judged to lie well outside the righteous camp.

I wonder what the two men talked about over their pork free dinner? Anyway, the totally unexpected outcome proved to be earth shattering. Zac, the despised, little quisling, decided to clean up his act by offering half of his wealth to the local poor. If he'd defrauded anyone, he generously promised to return *four times* the stolen cash to the victims of his scams. That ironic *if* could possibly lose him his ill-gained fortune.

What had triggered such a dramatic turn of events? Had Yeshua laid some religious guilt trip on the little, rich guy? I think not. What caused the radical change then? I believe it was simply the fact that Zac felt strangely comfortable in the the Nazarene's presence. He genuinely enjoyed the holy man's company, somehow feeling accepted for, perhaps, the first time in his chequered life.

Yeshua's perceptive reply to his criminal host's offer changed the religious scene forever.

Today salvation has been coming to this home.

What an amazing response. Neither rules, baptisms,

rituals, temple-attendance nor Torah study were required. By simply welcoming the Divine Presence resident within his teacher guest, the little loner had experienced a radical heart transplant; the Divine rewiring of his tortured psyche, leading to the generous surrender of his ill-gotten gains.

Surely the heart's welcome of Divine Presence in the form of Holy Breath is the antidote to the paralysing poison of any religious legalism or dysfunctional disharmony we may find ourselves locked into. The power to live free of such debilitating, psychological attachments resides in such a welcome, the outstretched arms of the human spirit.

May I suggest that salvation or wholeness is nothing to do with Christian creeds or alternative New Age belief systems, but rather in our openness to the whispering approach of Divine Love. I find it deeply disturbing that religious systems filed away under name of Yeshua, practice the very dualism of human classification that He,Himself, came to break down.

The believer/non believer Christian paradigm ultimately helps no-one, reinforcing instead the old self-righteous religious labelling of one's fellow-man. Surely we're all children of Yeshua's *Abba* whether we know it or not. It's certainly more fun knowing, so why don't we just enjoy our birthright and leave the *righteous* to do their own thing.

30

Yeshua Sayings That You Rarely Hear In Church ~ 2

"Father, forgive them for they are not being aware of anything they are doing."

Luke 23:34

What an amazing statement from the dying Galilean prophet as he suffers the horrendous trauma of Roman execution. The whole *Kingdom of God* thing now tragically appears to be another religious fad that's rapidly coming to an end; no sign of the big religious or political changes that many had forecasted; just a broken, tortured, body painfully hanging on a bizarrely effective execution device.

No wonder the Divine seemed to have deserted Him; the embarrassment for the Jewish God, Yahweh, would have been too much for Him to bear. Rather than a messenger of God, those few pietistic Jews, who could be bothered to stay around, believed the Nazarene to be cursed by the judging Jewish Divinity. Another false Messiah, another Apocalyptic dead-end.

The most radical of sayings to be heard from Yeshua's mouth, are uttered in the midst of the darkness of His now rapidly dwindling life. Desolation and despair are forcefully knocking at the door of His battered psyche, hoping to gain a victorious entrance. Three aspects of Yeshua's words blow me away. Let's look at each of them in turn.

Father

Yeshua's familial form of address to the Divine in such tragic circumstances seems like the delusional cry of a simpleton or madman. Like Job's comforters we attempt to put Him right.

"Listen here Yeshua. Your Abba God appears to have been a monster all along. So much for your sparrows and flowers of the field stories. I wonder if He knows how many ferocious military lashes you've suffered or the number of hairs on your now blood stained head?"

And yet the bond of intimacy between the broken prophet and His Divine commissioner remains; the trust of a faithful Son, despite the fast approaching end of His religious road. Refusing the judgement of self-righteous humanity, Yeshua clings to His Divinity for one last request.

Forgive them

What an earth shattering request from an innocent victim; one surely unique in the history of Roman crucifixion. The matter of fact, battle-hardened, execution squad must have been shocked by the Galilean's words. The remaining religious dignitaries probably didn't even hear them.

The Jewish Torah's advice of *an eye for an eye and a tooth for a tooth* was suddenly superseded by the dying Yeshua. <u>The days of the Law were over</u>. Loving one's neighbour as oneself had been finally fleshed out in this desperate, dramatic request. Yeshua appeared to confidently believe His own radical teaching to the bitter end. Yet, why should his military executioners and their politico-religious handlers receive such an outrageous forgiveness? Yeshua answers this deeply disturbing question for us in the following words:

For they are not aware of anything that they are doing

The Galilean claims that all who're directly or indirectly involved in His violent end are *unaware* of what they're doing. What a seemingly preposterous statement from the hanging preacher man! Didn't these experienced Roman soldiers know *exactly* what they were doing in nonchalantly carrying out their murderous orders? They'd done the deed often enough in the religion obsessed backwater of occupied Palestine. Did the Temple cult's High Priest and his academic advisors not realise what they'd initiated with Yeshua's arrest? Didn't Pilate in his role as hard-man Roman Governor know exactly how to stop a grass roots rebellion by taking out its populous charismatic leader?

According to Yeshua the answer was a great big *no*. All were mistaken, indeed radically asleep, regarding their role in His death; sleepwalking actors stumbling through their preassigned roles in the unfolding melodrama. Such an appalling lack of *awareness* proved to be the raison d'etre for Yeshua's request to the Divine for the forgiveness of their barbarous actions. He had forgiven them, now it was God's turn.

What a revelation of Divine Love in the victim's last words. Followers of the Nazarene were to later claim that the actions and words of their Master corresponded exactly to those of His *Abba* God. If true, then the shocking words of this dying utterance turns our concept of Divine justice on its head. Are we asleep and unaware of our *broken ego actions* as Yeshua seemed to suggest? Does free will only *appear* to operate within such a dreamlike state? Is personal responsibility a phantasm of our unaware consciousness?

If so, then the answer to our human predicament is an internal awakening, one in which dark scales fall away from our dimmed eyes, enabling us to see the Divine as an unconditionally loving Presence. Perhaps more importantly, we also wake up to our own deep level of psychic dysfunction, one in desperate need of reintegration and healing. Such an awakening experience, often following on from a painful transpersonal crisis, is the gracious gift of Divine Spirit; the beginning of our Journey Home.

As followers of Yeshua we too can forgive our enemies, knowing that they are unconscious victims of a demonic sleep; one from which we have been chosen to awake. Thankfully, Spirit Breath provides the dynamic resources required for such a seismic shift in our ego's dualistic mindset. Resigning from its self-appointed role as judge and jury is the key to our continuing psycho-spiritual freedom.

the veil of the temple was torn down the middle. Luke 23:45

the veil of the sanctuary was torn in two from top to bottom. Mark 15:38

And behold, the veil of the sanctuary was torn in two from top to bottom. The earth quaked, rocks were split, tombs were opened, and the bodies of many saints who had fallen asleep were raised.

And coming forth from their tombs after His resurrection, they entered the holy city and appeared to many.
  Matthew 27:51-53

* This marks the end of the sacrificial, scapegoating systems.

Yeshua Sayings That You Rarely Hear In Church ~ 3

"Is it not written in your law "I say you are gods"?"
John 10:34

    This little statement from Yeshua is truly a religious shocker. It provoked his stunned listeners to pick up some nearby stones in preparation for a ritualistic, sacred assassination. I suspect it might also have the same effect today among many of those who profess to be His followers; especially those who would argue His Divinity to the theological death. Let's have a look at the context in which these deeply disturbing and rarely proclaimed words were spoken.

    Yeshua was participating in the midst of an increasingly heated debate with Jewish religious experts in the outer courts of the Jerusalem Temple. He was being accused of blasphemy by those who dogmatically believed that *Yahweh* was the only Divine Presence in Jerusalem that cold, winter's day, holed up in the strange, dark, Temple room known as *the Holy of Holies*. Such a traditional belief played it safe, giving an ordered predictability to the Jewish method of approaching the Divine.

Yeshua's claim to be at One with His Divinity, the *Abba* Father, challenged the long established mindset of Jewish, religious and political life. Judaism was unique within the Mediterranean world for its monotheistic belief system. In Jewish eyes Yahweh was the only genuine divinity to be found in the complex, Greco-Roman marketplace of assorted deities. No wonder they were appalled and angered by the Nazarene rabbi's seemingly outrageous claims.

Suddenly, in an act of sheer brilliance, Yeshua pulls out of his spiritual repertoire, a respected but highly explosive text from Psalm 82.

I said "You are gods; and all of you sons of the Most High"

The Hebrew word *elohim,* translated *gods* in the above quote, is found over 2500 times in the Jewish Scriptures and almost always refers to the Jewish Divinity, even though it's the plural form of the Hebrew noun *El* meaning *the strong one*. There was no mistaking Yeshua's intention in quoting this text. He was claiming that the ancient Scriptures, the final authority for his learned listeners, suggested that humans were in some way *gods* or *divinities*, as children Sourced from their monotheistic God.

The much misunderstood, religious term, *Son of God,*

later placed on Yeshua by His future followers, had often referred to the ruling sovereign/High Priest during the early Temple period of Israel's formative sacred history; the one who annually stood alone before the *Cloud of Divine Presence* in the Holy of Holies. Was therefore, Yeshua's claim to be at One with the Father, so out of tune with Judaism's early mystical tradition? I believe not.

Unsurprisingly, Yeshua's revered audience didn't enjoy being theologically outplayed by the uneducated, itinerant, Galilean preacher, immediately attempting to arrest Him. Yet, as to date, Yeshua somehow once more made his mysteriously fortuitous escape. When it came *down to the wire*, the orthodox theologians chose their traditional belief system over Yeshua's empowering quotation from their supposedly, all-authoritative Scriptures. I believe that we spiritual seekers may find ourselves in a similar position today. Do we read Scriptures through the established spectacles of tradition and historical overlays rather than through those of a hungry and honest heart?

Clearly Yeshua used this little subversive text to justify His personal claim to be One with the Father and to shake up his listeners' perceptions of a separated and deeply jealous Divinity. Centuries later, early Church theologians, strongly influenced by the Greek philosophy of their day, formulated His shocking claim by introducing the intriguing doctrine of the Trinity.

I wonder though; did these Church Fathers stop short of

Yeshua's full disclosure? Did Yeshua's quote from Psalm 82 only justify His personal claim to divinity or was it intended to shed a radical new light on what it is to be fully human? Was he suggesting that humanity, once realigned with the *Abba* Father, has its god-likeness brought back into focus? What does it really mean to be made in the image of God? Have we a spark of Source Divinity buried deep within us during our seemingly humdrum, earthly sojourn? Are we living like paupers when we are meant to live, not like kings, but like gods? *Imago Dei* What are the implications of Yeshua's dream of a restored humanity? Here are my three suggestions:

We are creators.

Like the Divine Father, we possess a creative gene within our rewired psyches. The Divine gift of consciousness is the interactive screen on which we can project the desires of our realigned heart before seeing them manifest in our 3D world. We are part and parcel of the Father's creative expression, also able to flow in His creative power.

Why is it that what we fear usually comes upon us?

The answer is simple. It's the product of our dynamic, yet still unaligned, inner creative power. Fear, a negative form of creative flow produces its own dysfunctional manifestation. Once retuned by Spirit our harmonious psyche can once again reproduce the desires of Divine

Providence. Yeshua claimed that we'd do greater works than He achieved and He achieved some mind-boggling works. What an exciting way to live.

We are free to be.

One aspect of divinity is the ability to rise above all perceived reality. In other words, to be unaffected by the illusional storms of life; to see beyond the stresses of our ego battles and to detach from the desire control of others by confidently declaring *'I am that I am'*, the very nature of our Divine Source.

We are channels of Divine Love.

God, we are simply told, is Love. If we, like Yeshua, are at one with His *Abba* God, sharing a revived spark of His Source nature, then surely it is Love that dwells within us as the Divine deposit. Could our *godness* be this Spirit essence? Are we not designed to love as God loves, unconditionally and without return? Like a repaired pipe, we once again have the capacity to carry the flow of Divine compassion and healing. Could St. Paul's claim of *'being in The Anointed One'*, (Christ or Messiah), be a much greater revelation than we've hereto grasped? Can it not signify our adoption into divinity as those awakened and consumed by Divine Love?

"You are gods; and all of you sons of the Most High."

A return to Source, a return to the Heart from which we sprang as space-time began its illusionary dance in the Mind of God.

32

Yeshua Sayings That You Rarely Hear In Church ~ 4

"For you took away the "key of knowledge". You yourselves didn't enter and you hindered the ones entering in."

Luke 11:52

In this provocative statement, Yeshua once more turns the full force of the Divine spotlight onto the prevalent religious mindset of His day, indeed, onto the hidden mindset of all religious systems throughout the ages. The sacred skeleton in the cupboard can no longer remain dressed up in the pseudo-respectability that it cleverly attempts to clothe itself in.

What exactly is this *key of knowledge* that Yeshua claims Judaism's religious top brass were holding back from the common people of His day? In order to answer such a crucial question we need to examine the context of the Nazarene's debate with His Jewish elders.

Yeshua has just fired both barrels at the number of excessive laws extrapolated onto the Torah by the Jewish Scribes. In other words, He was confronting the timeless issue of religious legalism that always reduces the big, spiritual picture to the minutiae of pietistic duty.

Yet, in the ensuing discussion, Yeshua unearths a much darker and sinister problem that lies as the foundation stone of all religious systems viz. violence and its accompanying hypocrisy; the hidden elephant in every holy of holies. The revelation of violence, lying at the heart of our commonly perceived route to holiness, is, I believe, the key referred to by the Galilean prophet-teacher; the key that opens the door to a totally new perception of the Divine Nature.

In first century Palestine the construction of tomb memorials to the prophets of past generations helped consolidate a much threatened, Jewish national identity, in the face of Roman oppression and occupation. The religious authorities in Jerusalem *appeared* to honour the pioneering spokesmen of their embryonic faith whilst paradoxically honouring their forefathers who'd murdered them. Yeshua decides to go straight for the sacred jugular in exposing the blatant hypocrisy of His fellow debaters by claiming that all prophets throughout human history, (Abel to Zechariah), had been murdered by the status quo religious representatives of their day. Luke 11:37-54

Yeshua's previous declaration that we cannot serve two masters appeared not to have registered with His supposedly learned audience. The religious violence of the past was repeatedly being hushed up, indeed, literally whitewashed over on the victims' grand memorial tombs. A good gloss has always been painted over such religiously motivated murders.

The Nazarene, ominously a prophet Himself, dared to expose the violent spirit that continued to underlie the religious game since the dawn of human history. He well and truly succeeded in flushing this destructive genie out of its shiny, sacred lamp, thus determining His own particularly tragic, yet deeply prophetic destiny.

'You are sons of your father who was a murderer from the beginning' elsewhere exploded the early Jewish myth of a violent, angry God, the father in question being the *Satan* or *Adversary* of skewed human desire. No wonder Yeshua's listeners immediately attempted to respond with violence, ironically proving the truth of His claims regarding their dubious spiritual parentage. *John 8:44, 39-59*

The murder of Abel, the first brother, is a telling prototype of all future religious rivalry and its resulting violence; the striking out of sacred jealousy birthed by a dysfunctional perception of the Divine. A *founding murder* misinterpreted as the result of a Divine rejection; a subtle mechanism that regularly keeps the religious show on the road.

"For God and Ulster"

This paramilitary slogan for war in my deeply divided homeland of Northern Ireland, says it all. The Divine has been mistakenly woven into the very fabric of human violence since Cain lashed out at his innocent sibling. Jealous of Divine approval, the sons of God go to war, carrying their dualistic Deity deep within their wounded, love starved psyches.

No matter how effective the cover up, the violence at the heart of religion will, given time, always rear its ugly head - like a jack-in-the-box that must eventually pop up. *'Look how they love one another'* has become the taunt of non-believers worldwide as they witness the often bloody rivalry at the heart of all sacrificial religion.

As we all know, this radical revelation of religious violence by Yeshua quickly resulted in His own tragic, but not totally unexpected murder. Dressed up in the guise of politico-religious expediency; the Satanic genie had hit back in its time-honed modus operandi. Further unmasked through the Crucifixion of its Divine whistle-blower, the stunned violent godfather quickly struck back by insidiously dressing the risen Victim in violent apparel of His own. A perverse but deeply effective diabolical counter-play: a Father and Saviour Son who'd dispatch non believers to a place of eternal torment for their non-belief. A violent God now ridding Himself of violent men.

May I suggest that, like its Jewish predecessor, the religion of Yeshua also does a *tomb job* on its quickly dispatched prophets. Is this *key of knowledge* still important in our walk with the Divine? I believe so. The nature of religion, no matter what the brand, is still essentially the same; under its respectable Jesus layer lurks a hidden sibling rival that negates the very message of the Nazarene viz. a Divine Love that unconditionally welcomes and accepts all.

Thankfully, Spirit Breath, the inner Voice of such a Love can always be heard, whispering, far from the violent battlefields of religious systems, the fractured, dualistic world of *them and us*. Let's constantly be on our guard; may we never mistake the Way of the whitewashed Tomb for the Living Way of Yeshua, the Lamb Victim, slain before space- time began.

33

The Inner Void

One of the strangest rooms in the history of religious experience was the Jewish *Holy of Holies*. At first an enclosed room within Judaism's portable skin tent or *Tabernacle*, it was later incorporated as the sacred focal point of Solomon's First Temple in Jerusalem.

What was this small, mysterious, cubic room all about? Has it anything to teach us in our 21st century journey into the Divine?

Perhaps the most surprising fact regarding the holy cube was its sparsity of furniture. Within Solomon's Temple it housed the famous *Ark of the Covenant*, a gold lined box containing two stone tablets inscribed with the Ten Commandments, commonly believed to have been handed to the Jewish leader Moses by *Yahweh* Himself. The gilded lid of the Ark, known as the mercy-seat, was where Yahweh's mystical cloud Presence, or *Shekinah* was said to reside during His rare manifestations to the Temple's High Priest. The Ark's unusual contents also included Aaron's miraculously flowering rod, and a jar of manna, representing respectively, the Jewish deliverance from Egyptian slavery and the *Bread of Life* that had kept them alive during their nomadic wanderings.

In the subsequent Second Temple of Yeshua's time the *Holy of Holies* was simply, yet perhaps profoundly, an empty room, following the disappearance of The Ark and other related religious artefacts during the Babylonian Empire's earlier destruction of Jerusalem.

This small, dark, holy room was strange location into which, on *Yom Kippur, The Day of Atonement,* Judaism's most sacred day, the somewhat mysterious High Priest entered to meet Yahweh face to face, as Moses had done all those centuries before. Such a meeting with the Divine in a constricted, dark space, lit only by the Light of Shekhinah Presence may have implications for our own inner life.

Perhaps we too, dwelling in our own empty, inner darkness, can be likened to Judaism's most sacred space? When life has been drained of all superficiality through our descent into confusion and despair, when we sit alone in the seeming singularity of our inner humanity, when love seems far away and human or religious trust completely irrelevant, what is left? *Nothing, or Ultimate Reality?*

In this silent, and often painful void of the human heart is their not space for such a Divine manifestation, our own personal Day of Atonement, a unique appointment with Sacred Oneness? Doesn't a Shekhinah Presence come to surprise us in our intense sense of aloneness, causing us, like the High Priest of ancient times, to fall on our faces in awe and bewilderment? Isn't our only hope the transforming Presence that causes our face to shine with Spirit, like that of Moses, after our contact in the desert of solitude?

Yes, but where do we encounter such a Divinity, if it can be experienced at all?

It's certainly not experienced in the mind where conceptual truth is mistakenly worshipped as Ultimate Reality. Many Yeshua followers choose to fall short of their birthright by settling for doctrinal knowledge dressed up as Truth. This pale, lifeless shadow of Divine Presence promises much but ultimately leaves the human spirit still thirsting for Life. Theologians and philosophers frantically search through the analytical maze of supposed free thought hoping to nail such a Presence down, straightjacketing it with the rigorous chains of religious theory.

Fortunately Divine Spirit mischievously sidesteps the vain clutches of such academics, choosing instead to meet the common man in his inner chamber, the 'I' room, one designed for such an intimate encounter. As the defences of our collective, survival sub-personalties or ego crumble, their social and material supports tumbling into extinction, a door opens into the darkness of our confusion; here we stand, stripped naked of self-assurance and, most definitely, alone. As we wait in deep despair for the Divine Light, the comforting energy of our Creator Parent, our

Way Beyond The Blue

Source, the very One from whence we've come, we sincerely doubt whether He'll show.

A tear of release falls mournfully from our eye, unknown to us, the first harbinger of His determined approach. Thankfully, a Light appears, as surely as day follows night, but only once the gift of darkness has carried out its summary execution of our enslaving ego. Only then, does all make sense; when spirit embraces Spirit in the ecstatic Dance of liberation.

So, on our journey into the unknown, let's not be afraid of our inner world, our *Holy of Holies*, our Divine meeting place, for to such a place we will return on our parting breath. Better to get familiar with it now I reckon.

34

Friends

Last night I'd one of my recovering religious junkie dreams. They seem to pop up every so often, to kindly inform me that my fragile, yet healing psyche still carries the scars of previous religious practice. Anyway, here is my dream:

I was in a group of religio-spiritual seekers, in the centre of which stood my old pastor Jake. He seemed to be surrounded by scaffolding as if something was about to be built around him. The other folk present appeared to be looking admiringly into his eyes. Suddenly, in my little nocturnal drama I shouted out a question to Jake.

"Jake, before I gave you the position of my pastor you were my friend. Do you think such a role has damaged our friendship? Am I still your friend?"

In the dream I felt glad that I'd asked the question, getting it off my chest so to speak before I suddenly woke up to be greeted by the damp, dull, Lincolnshire morning.

I've been meditating on my dream today, trying to discover its subliminal message. Here's what's come to me thus far:

I believe the dream's central message concerns the insidious power of religious roles on the individual spiritual seeker. Let's explore the place of such roles within the psycho-spiritual journey, and compare them with a radical statement from Yeshua, one boxed into the ultimate religious role of *Saviour of the World*.

> "No longer am I terming you slave servants for the slave servant isn't aware of anything his lord is doing. Yet, I've declared you friends, for all that I hear coming from my Father I make known to you."
> *John 15:15*

Yeshua was born into a world packed with religious roles; Jewish Priests, Lawyers, Preacher - Prophets, and Rabbis populated the Judean countryside as the Roman military brutally kept the lid on a simmering Nationalistic fervour. All good Rabbis had their slave servants, or disciples, who literally surrounded their masters, hanging onto every word they said, hoping to catch a little bit of their spiritual enlightenment. Yeshua Himself appears to have used this model of training in His early ministry. Peter and company, by leaving behind their fishing careers to plug into the new Yeshua following, hoped to encounter something of the Divine in their unusual master. Indeed as time passed they were convinced they'd hit the jackpot, by identifying Him as the long-awaited Mashiach, the anointed military priest-king who'd dispatch the hated Romans for good. Roles came thick and fast as Yeshua asked His closest slave-servants who people thought He was; a reincarnated Elijah or John the Baptiser being their preferred choices. *Matthew 16:15*

Yet, at the end of His three years training course, Yeshua comes out with the above statement. Peter, James and John along with the other members of His inner circle were released from their perceived roles as slave servants. Yeshua was revealing that He was a different kind of rabbi, one who trains His spiritual band of seekers into the true nature of spirituality, a friendship with the Divine. Once introduced to Spirit, the Voice and energy of God flow directly to the disciple, taking them from the starting rung of the spiritual ladder, the place of roles, onto the higher levels of intimacy with the Divine; the place of union and ultimate unity with the Other.

In my own experience, the Spirit Presence loves to dwell in the mutual vulnerability that true friendship can provide; the place of sacred space; where two or three come together, not to do religion, but to open up their broken humanity to one another, in an authentic spirit of humility. Religion and its multi-layered power plays are addicted to holy roles. Let's step out from our role-play box; we might just bump into Divine Love, patiently waiting for us.

If we've friends like this, we'll find ourselves falling out of love with sanctimonious sacred cameos and closer to the One who is closer than any friend. Why don't we start by befriending our *Self* today? As a result Divinity will suddenly manifest those who can safely sail alongside us on the Journey Home.

Dylan Morrison

35

Anam Cara ~ Soul Friend: Part 1

The ancient Celts had a very different world view to that of 21st man. Having been spared the rigid classification of scientific method these ancestors of ours saw the world as a Oneness through which Mystery shines it multi-coloured rays. When you and I suddenly notice three Wild Geese flying overhead, we admire them as wonders of the Natural world. The Celts would have interpreted their unexpected appearance much differently, seeing it as a Divine confirmation of the Spirit's Presence and guidance on the Way.

In such a mystical tradition the notion of an *Anam Cara* or *Soul Friend* was birthed; one to accompany us on our deeply personal Journey of Discovery. A friend, yes, but not *just* a friend. A fellow traveller on the River of Spirit, a companion to feed the Soul and encourage us Homeward to Source and the Celtic Land of Eternal Youth. In this chapter I will focus on the general concept of friendship; the *Soul* or *Spiritual* friend I will tackle in Chapter 39.

Thankfully we all have, or have had, friends during our

earthly sojourn. Most friendships blossom, flourish and die as life's changing circumstances carry us far apart. If we dare to examine our past friendships more closely, we might shockingly discover that they were merely mutual appreciation trade offs whereby each of us received something from the other that we strongly craved. Once we or our friend received the desired psychological goodies or found a more dependable or, dare I say it, a more gullible supplier, the friendship either faded away or exploded into all out war.

I suspect that much of what we label as friendship is, in fact, a codependency operating within a mutual desire matrix; one that often ends up with tears being shed over the corpse of a broken relationship. What then is the nature of genuine friendship? I believe it to be an open relationship between two individuals who've realised that the answers to their emotional and psychological needs lie, not with each other, but with a common Source.

As we saw in the previous chapter Yeshua appears to have travelled with His band of disciples for somewhere between two to three years. A long time for a group of feisty mature men to have lived within a well defined Master-Disciple matrix. Were Peter, James and John friends with Yeshua during this period? Apparently not, according to Yeshua Himself. In John's account of their life together it was only in the latter days of their togetherness that Yeshua unilaterally declared them friends. Why?

The Nazarene suggests that the men were now His *friends* because they'd learnt to keep these two commandments:

> *Loving the Divinity with all their emotional and psychological sense of Being*
>
> *Loving their neighbours as their own Selves*

In other words, through daily contact with Yeshua, the disciples had finally realised that they were freely accepted by Divine Love without fear of a mood swing celestial thunderbolt.

Birthed from this revolutionary revelation a surging Love flowed back towards Divine Source, the individual's essential Self, and outwards in the direction of the apparent other. A realignment of the creative Love Triangle, A Holy circle, once again complete. Such an understanding of Divine Love reopened up the Edenic Friendship between God and Man; the Master Servant relationship being consigned to the annuls of religious effort.

Interestingly, when the role of discipleship is zealously emphasised in the modern religious context do we not catch a telling glimpse of a kindergarten level of God understanding? Is not true friendship that connection of spirit that flows effortlessly between two or more enlightened or *born from above* Souls. Like a good marriage, are they not *made in Heaven*?

36

Anam Cara ~ Soul Friend: Part 2

In the last chapter I looked at the topic of friendship – what it is and what it is not. We discovered that much of what occurs in relationships, benignly termed *friendships* is no more than a mutual exchange of emotional goods, an attachment or agreement if you like between *soul* traders. As soon as one party acquires all their psychological needs or finds a more productive source elsewhere the so called friendship comes to an end.

An unexpected breakdown in the cosy world of friendships is, paradoxically, the time when true, authentic friendships have the opportunity to appear. As the drug-like, psychological attachment is painfully broken the individual concerned is open, perhaps for the first time, to the *Other, the Source t*hat paradoxically lies within and without the human heart.

Once such an awakening occurs, others with similar experiences begin to gravitate towards the newly enlightened soul with the purpose of sharing his/her life. Thus a friendship is formed, not one dependant on the mutual stroking of fragmented egos, but one based upon a common life flow from the Other. Needless to say, such relationships tend to avoid the subliminal manipulation and power play games of the majority of human interactions. Instead, both parties are content to eat of the Father's table and channel their inner sense of Divine acceptance outwards, towards the other.

So what then is a Gaelic, *Anam Cara*; a *Soul Friend*? Is it more than the authentic friend discussed above? I believe so! In my personal experience a Soul Friend is, if you like, a Special Forces operative in the Friendship Army; indeed, a specialist Paratrooper to boot. Please let me explain.

Our Soul Friends generally drop into our lives from out of nowhere, just at the right time, appearing to act out a pre-scripted, heavenly drama. Unlike our more conventional friends, the Anam Cara appears to have had an almost identical experience to ourselves in their search for Self and Divine Love. This close identification is manifested in the totally unconditional acceptance that flows between the two individuals concerned. Such a friendship doesn't appear to require high maintenance, the hard work having already been carried out in a higher plane of existence.

Subliminal rivalry, the hidden killer of many friendships cannot easily deploy its death grip on such special friendships, both parties possessing a great immunity to the highly destructive inter-personal virus.

Like a Special Forces operative the Soul Friend has a finely honed set of skills ready to bring into the friendship mix at short notice. These are:

Vision – a clear view of the Big Picture; the ability to see why the friendship exists and where they are both heading in the Divine Journey.

Wisdom – a seemingly effortless flow of Spirit knowledge for encouraging their friend on the Way; the practical outworking of Divine Love in the individual's day to day life.

Compassion – the ability to feel the other's pain in shadow valleys and the will to help in any way possible.

Trust – the unusual ability that allows Divine Love to carry them on the River of Life; a quality that ignites the same reaction in their friend.

Is an Anam Cara a spiritual director or master to their disciple friend? I believe not. There is no master-disciple dichotomy in one's relationship with a Soul Friend. In other words Soul Friends come in pairs, Special Forces friends for each other, thus avoiding the dangers of control in the mutual relationship flow.

The unusual characteristic regarding our Anam Cara is that neither time nor geographical relocation diminishes the nature of the friendship; it appears that the spirit resonance or vibration that knits such souls is permanent, ready to be reactivated when required. Like the proven psychic connection between identical twins the respective Soul Friends appear to share a spiritual DNA. Hence the fear of losing our Anam Cara is groundless; they just don't go away, unlike many of our passing friendships.

Divine Love realises that the path to Self Knowledge and Divine Communion can be a lonely one. Indeed, each of us must ultimately make that journey alone but thankfully there is help along the way.

As we open our hearts and look up for he/she may just be about to parachute onto our path, ready for the Way ahead. An angel by any other name.

I would like to dedicate this chapter to my personal Anam Cara, Stephen Hill, a true Soul Brother, living in beautiful New Zealand, a world away from my Lincolnshire home. May Divine Presence cover and saturate both him and his wee family.

Way Beyond The Blue

37

Two-Way Traffic: Part 1

What a weird and yet wonderful journey life is. Most of the time we don't know which way to turn or even which direction we're supposed to be heading in. The confusion is all-encompassing; both the religio-spiritual and agnostic-cum-atheistic tribes get caught out by the sheer dizziness of it all. Is there a road map that can help us make sense of the Journey Home, wherever Home is supposed to be? Here is my humble offering to the human GPS dilemma.

The simpler the road map the easier it is for us to get our bearings on our seemingly complex pilgrimage through space-time.

I believe that life may be viewed as a psycho-spiritual continuum along which we travel. Paradoxically, at each end of such a continuous path lie our chosen destinations.

At one end lies the Divine, the Source of our being, the creative womb from which we originally burst forth. At the other end lies our Soul Self or psyche, the total sum of our consciousness, both known and unknown. Where are we at any one instant in our sojourn? May I suggest that we're either heading towards the Divine or towards our Self.

In this chapter I want to look at the Journey towards the Soul Self for those who've already encountered their version of the Divine. In the following chapter I'll examine the Journey of those who've encountered a measure of the Soul Self prior to their Divine destination.

If we're honest most of us past or present religious devotees haven't much of an idea with respect to who we are. All we *know* is that God loves us to some extent depending on how we perceive the nature of that Love viz. conditional or unconditional. Unfortunately such an *us* is traditionally identified as a *redeemed sinner*, one who's been lucky enough to have accepted the Divine offer of reconciliation. If we've undergone a spiritual experience during our religious conversion, we instantaneously enjoy a new identity that initiates us into the supposed, mystical *Body of Christ*. Before long we're urgently encouraged by the faithful to sign up for its flesh and blood manifestation, the religious organization reverentially referred to as a *good church*.

Unfortunately, our newly discovered identity as a child of the Divine is all too quickly quickly absorbed and ultimately replaced by an insidious substitute Self Image, that of *the committed and loyal church member*. Soon our old non-religious Self is deprogrammed, reckoned dead and buried deep within the secure vaults of our lower unconscious. Our zealous new religious persona, now firmly installed in the psycho-spiritual driving seat, looks forward to a bright and ever blessed future.

Depending on the nature of our religious observance, such a paradigm shift generally works for a while. Empowered with an ardent energy we celebrate our new life, as defined through the theological spectacles of our particular sect. Does such a process deny the authentic nature of our initial and perhaps continuing encounters with the *Other*? Surprisingly as it may seem, I don't believe so.

Certainly Divine Spirit is now severely hampered in the healing and restoration of our true Soul Self, having a powerful new religious member of the fragmented psyche to deal with. Further repressed by the subtle stoicism of *sacrificial* teaching, our wounded Soul lies trapped in the darkness of our inner prison, awaiting permission to emerge into the Light.

During such a period of denial, the *usurper* or *religious ego* puts a brave face on things, cranking up the amount of blood, sweat and tears it can muster to convince itself that it is indeed a new creature. Down below our chained Soul Self shuffles around in the basement of our unconscious waiting for true liberation and acceptance.

Where is Divine Spirit during this relentless religious performance? Simply waiting for, and yet orchestrating events towards, one end viz. *Honesty*. Honesty is the Divinely gifted key that unlocks the padlock of our denial. How do we get to that place of honesty? In my own experience it came through the brokenness of a transpersonal crisis; a stripping away of the religious Self and its false confidence. My personal key to freedom was cleverly placed by Spirit at the end of my rope, a place of seeming abandonment and total nervous exhaustion.

The Divine embrace of one's recently released soul-psyche parallels that of the Father's in Yeshua's revealing tale of the Prodigal Son. Only when he came to him*self* was the religiously trained boy able to run back home into the arms of Divine Love. Was his previous rebellion just a frantic search for Soul Self, the missing piece of his Journey's jigsaw? Does a genuine sense of Self only emerge once we've suffered the burn out of our desire driven ego? I suspect so.

Which end of the life-continuum am I presently heading towards? If Soul Self, then I must remember that, contrary to much religious teaching, it too is welcomed at the Divine table. Let the merriment begin!

38

Two-Way Traffic: Part 2

Previously, I considered those who've encountered the Divine in some shape or form, perhaps early on in life, only to later set out on a desperate search for their Soul-Self. For some this entails a radical breaking away from their previous religious identity in order to begin the new journey; for others the search can be incorporated within the paradigm of their present religio-spiritual box. In this chapter I'd like to address my thoughts to those of us who've never experienced an encounter with *Other*, at least not knowingly, only to travel through life trying to find a satisfying sense of Self.

As youngsters, our sense of *I* or *Me* greatly depends on the authentication of our Being through the mirroring of unconditional love by significant others, usually our parents. The developing Self continually seeks such approval from those who claim, in their better moments, to *love* us. In a Utopian world of perfect parents and a non judgemental environment, this would clearly result in our well-rounded, harmonious sense of 'I' that would, in turn, flow outwards towards others with unconditional love. Yet, it would appear that, no matter how frequently the desired parental reflection of *You're OK* occurs, no-one can replicate the constancy of Divine Love due to their own level of psychic wounding. Having faced the resulting trauma of conditional love and its inherent message of rejection, our developing psyches immediately create defence mechanisms in order to cope with the pain of our perceived non-being.

These multiple defenders take the form of *sub-personalities*, fragmented splinters of the developing psyche that dramatically split off from our still fragile sense of I, following the traumas of *non authentication*. Such sub-personalities are extremely powerful, with a high level of ingenuity that attempts to dull the pain of our parent's guilty verdict. Over the course of our formative years, these significant, little sub-personalities coalesce as *familial clusters*, or *psychic gangs*, that defend our now highly sensitive Self against repetitions of our initial or primal wounding. As a result of such a tragic, psychic mobilisation, we head off, deeply handicapped, into the unknown of adolescence under the command of our recently fractured Soul-Self ~ the *ego*.

Fight, flight or *freeze* has become the order of the day as the world is radically re-interpreted as an unsafe and dangerous territory for the unwary individual to dwell. Ego frantically sets out on its restless search for a secure hiding place, piling up as much money, sex or power as it can on the tortuous journey called life. Sadly, many of us run, like a hapless hamster on a treadmill, round our fear filled circuits until death itself grants us a terrifying, if highly effective, reprieve from the tyranny of the ever entrenched ego.

Others of us, finally disarmed by a seemingly endless series of transpersonal crises, collapse alongside our exhausted egos, wondering, for perhaps the first time, who or what we essentially *are*. The result of much self-induced suffering, the momentarily stunning of the ego is a rare opportunity for deep reflection on the frantic freeway we call life. At moments like this, many of us dramatically change the direction and pace of our walk towards meaning. A fleeting glimpse of a healed and integrated psyche is tantalizingly held before us as we begin the quest for a new Holy Grail, the Divine gift of Self. Such a search usually results in a change of circumstances viz. a new job, new relationships, new attitudes to money, leisure time etc. For some the adjustments are moderate, for others earth-shattering. I see those in the latter category as eventually heading onto one of two following paths:

Monist philosophy or *Psychotherapy*

Many of us coming from a non-religious background are attracted to the Oneness message of much modern spirituality. The rapid growth of the Mind, Body, Spirit genre over the last 20 years or so is nothing less than breathtaking. Western interpretations of Eastern Monist philosophy such as Buddhism have provided a strong sense of Self for those seeking a rediscovery of their essential essence. The journey within, as practised through meditation or mindfulness, detaches the individual from the vestiges of their fragmented ego, finding A Self that is in touch with all things, indeed, appears to be All Things. Who or what is this observer Self that such monists highly value? Where did it come from and what is its nature?

Others choose the demanding route developed by the fathers of 20th century psychotherapy and its post modern offshoots. Having had personal experience of *Roberto Assagioli's* 'Psychosynthesis' therapy I shall briefly outline its designated journey towards a new awareness of Self.

Here the unconscious cellar, in which our sub-personalities make camp, is examined with the aid of the talking therapies and their visual derivatives. Discovering our so-called *hidden demons* and exposing them to the authenticated acceptance of the therapist slowly begins the reintegration of our fragmented inner community. Thus begins a much needed demobilization for the defenders of the wounded Self. If the unconditional love that the underdeveloped soul has craved since birth is now freely available, then the paralysing protection of the sub-personality is no longer required. Now discharged from duty, the psychic gang clusters are warmly embraced, one by one, thereby deactivating their power to cause havoc in the darkness of our repressed memories and emotions.

The naming of our sub-personalities and the tracing of their birth circumstances rob them of their previously hidden, compulsive power. Like the post exorcism Gadarene demoniac before them they now sit *sane and in their right mind* ready to reintegrate into our internal psychic family. Gathering around the table of the Soul, each reformed sub-personality is now welcomed and embraced for its dynamic gifts and vital contribution to the psychic Whole.

Who acts as host to this long sought after reconciliation? It is, I believe, the newly recognized *I*, the very same observer of Oneness within the Monist tradition. This rediscovered Transpersonal or Higher Self eventually internalises the external authenticator role of the therapist, who has hot-wired the whole process of our inner healing. What is the nature and origin of this *I* that plays such an essential role in the recovery and reintegration of the fractured psyche? Let's find out in the next chapter!

Dylan Morrison

39

Two-Way Traffic: Part 3

In Parts 1 & 2 we looked at our individual journey of discovery towards a rewarding sense of authentic *Self*. Following the painful, yet essential, exposure of the *fractured psyche* or *ego* the seeker tentatively begins to enter a healing process whereby their *sub-personalities* or *psychic splinters* are reintegrated into a wholesome community know as the Soul. We observed that, for some, this healing process may require dramatic intervention in the form of:

Monist philosophy or *Psychotherapy*

Both of these seemingly different approaches to the healing method have, surprisingly, much in common, viz. the *non judgemental observer* or *authentic unifying centre*.

Within the* Monist tradition this new kid on the block is internal; the One who views the rantings and ravings of the ego as a neutral and somewhat detached observer. Within Psychotherapy, this important role is initially external with

*and contemplation, 'prayer' of the heart', Western & Eastern meditation, prayer taught by Desert Abbas & Ammas AND

the therapist acting as a loving greeter to the somewhat nervous, emerging sub-personalities. The goal of all such successful therapy is to eventually transfer this vital job description to the latent *I am* within.

I believe that these parallel approaches are, largely unknown to each other, taking the individual on the same inner journey; the destination being a mysterious introduction to our internal *other*. Who or what is this *one* whom we meet, deep within the caverns of our Being? I suspect it to be *spirit-breath*, that divine essence who accompanies us through birth into our world of consciousness and matter. A fruit of the Divine Tree, a spark from the Divine Fire, the spirit birthed by the One in whom we live and move and have our Being is amazingly the *real us*. Acts 17:28

During our roller coaster Journey, this embodied spirit has been waiting patiently for our fractured psyche to run its course; for the energetic ego to fall exhausted in a desperate act of surrender. This *Transpersonal Self* or *I am* dwells on the boundary of two worlds, like the border post between two realms of Reality; the gatekeeper to Ultimate Source, to Divine Love itself. I believe it sits at the apex of our Higher Unconscious, the foothills of the mysterious Mountain Range that we call Divinity.

Once we've encountered our spirit essence, we can never be the same again. For this stranger within introduces us to the One from whom we came viz. Holy

centering prayer And Welcoming prayer!

Breath/Wind/Spirit, who like a Royal Prince sweeps through our spirit gate to flood us with a deep sense of Homecoming. The long awaited connection is now complete as we're embraced in the arms of Love, a torrential Love that desires to fill our parched psyche-Soul.

Divine flow is restored; the dynamic intimacy of Source realigns every fibre of our Being. Our restored Soul family once more reflects the Unity of our spirit core, the *I am*, who in turn reflects the very nature of the One, referred to by Yeshua as *Abba,* Father. Even our frail bodies, once stressed and damaged by our previously warring sub-personalities, take their place in the Divine Life flow, as a growing sense of health and equilibrium replace the previous physical manifestations of our diseased Soul. Now that's what I call *Salvation*.

40

Will I Or Won't I? ~ Part 1

One of the most confusing, yet potentially empowering elements of the human psyche is the *Will* - the part of us that, at a superficial glance, seems to control our lives. For those of us who've entered onto the spiritual path, following an encounter with *Other* a few pertinent questions regarding the role of Will may need answered. These are:

How does the Divine Will interface with human will?

What psycho-spiritual role does our will play within the complexity of our internal wiring?

In this chapter, I want to explore some possible answers to these two questions through the medium of parable. So here goes.

Once upon a time, there lived a dynamic entrepreneur named *Grace Sophia*; a charismatic inventor who'd come up with some of the most mind-boggling masterpieces ever seen in the world of form. People said that they couldn't remember a time when Grace wasn't doing her thing.

Appearing ageless, she'd been at the top of her game for as long as the businesses market had existed.

Grace's pride and joy was her flagship company Self Incorporated. It's meteoric rise had taken it straight to the coveted number one spot in the field of Cosmic marketing. The opposition was flabbergasted, totally blown out of the water. With multi-directional creativity bursting from her fingertips, Grace soon handed over the oversight of her beloved enterprise to her newly appointed talented CEO, *Ruach*. Appearing to be a chip off the old block in the eyes of many of Grace's competitors, the newly appointed executive exuded a pioneer spirit mixed with a deep love for the product and his workforce.

Employed by Self as its day-to-day, hands-on manager was *Will*, an altogether different kettle of fish from both Grace and her delegated protégé, Ruach. Decisive and with great organizational skill, Will complemented the flamboyant visionary gifts of his new CEO. Corporate commentators interested in the fortunes of Self Inc., soon observed that the boardroom pairing seemed like a match made in heaven.

Self's dedicated workforce was, undoubtedly, the hidden jewel in the company's fortunes; a well motivated group of skilled artisans who thoroughly enjoyed working for the Sophia brand, rolling her exemplary products off the production line, as fast as she could invent them.

At first, all went well for this most innovative of

companies, mainly as a result of the exemplary levels of industrial harmony that permeated all aspects of its corporate operations. Sadly, however, it was not to last. One Monday morning, Will received a call from Ruach's wife informing him that her husband had been taken ill overnight and rushed to the intensive care unit of the city hospital. A severe heart attack had been diagnosed. Ruach's doctors had recommended that he take an indefinite break from Self for the foreseeable future. Grace had already authorised Will's promotion to acting CEO of her leading company. However, news of Ruach's plight hit the workforce badly. Within a few chaotic weeks, questioning and dissension began to break out on the Self shop floor. A disconcerting rivalry began to spread, virus like, among the previously harmonious and united team.

Will himself, having been a decisive manager when yoked with the inspirational Ruach, began to have trouble making simple decisions. Uncharacteristically, insecure in his new CEO position, he now called upon the most vocal members of the shop floor for their advice. Unfortunately, such consultations became the battlefield for warring hotheads, with Will being dragged to and fro across the fractious terrain of the workers' Soul. Now a shadow of his former self, a puppet pulled by the all too obvious strings of his workers' fragmented desire, Will was being slowly executed by the rumblings of those supposedly in his care.

It didn't take long before the topsy-turvy situation

brought the once proud company to its knees. As output fell, Self began to tumble-down the market share rankings. The once decisive Will had, unwittingly, surrendered his position of responsibility to the strong personalities within the now rampantly rivalrous workforce. Word of Self's tragic demise quickly got back to Grace. Sitting in the numbed silence the matriarchal entrepreneur shed a slow, mournful tear, before reaching for her cell phone. It was time to exercise her Will.

To be continued

41

Will I Or Won't I ~ Part 2

Within twenty four hours, Grace was sitting in the CEO's luxury office at Self Incorporated's national headquarters. In front of her stood an anxious Will, accompanied by a young stranger who looked vaguely familiar.

"You can relax Will; I'm here to take a big load off your shoulders."

Will wasn't quite sure what his boss meant, tending to believe that he was about to take his place among the great mass of unemployed that walked the streets of broken humanity.

'Come here', Grace whispered firmly, beckoning the shell-shocked executive closer with an outstretched arm.

What happened next was not what Will had envisioned. Getting up from her classy CEO chair, Grace flung her arms around Will as she unexpectedly began to sob.

"Will, thank you for trying to keep Self afloat in the absence of Ruach."

A stunned Will automatically fell to his knees, wailing deeply as he further collapsed into a crumpled heap on the luxury pile carpet. A long, angst-filled cry eerily pierced the surreal atmosphere as Will felt the burdens of the past months fall away, replaced by a lightness that came flooding back into his empty, dark being.

Glancing upwards, Will could just make out the form of the stranger leaning over him as he became embarrassingly aware of his salty tears trickling their way onto his parched tongue. Somehow he sensed a familiar energy flowing from this man, the one now embracing him in his brokenness. Where had he felt this psychic connection before?

"Will, I want to introduce you to someone; meet Rukah, Ruach's younger brother. He'll be taking over his position as from today."

Yes, now it all fell into place; the strange knowing and even stranger flow of energy. Will had first felt it, the day Self had been launched; a warm introductory handshake from Ruach being the channel for the empowering Life surge. During their time together in management it had never left him. As Will rose tentatively to his feet, a new management team was birthed that would restore the fortunes of Self Incorporated. Will's gifts would come back into play alongside the new boy Rukah and the wise oversight of Grace Sophia.

"And now gentlemen, let's go see my workers. Will, you

Way Beyond The Blue

lead the way."

As the three executives walked onto the shop floor, the employees of Self Inc. couldn't believe their eyes. Never in their wildest dreams had they expected to see their founder Grace once more walking among them. Their hearts were pulled this way and that by the turbulence of conflicting emotions; the fear of losing their jobs and the sheer relief at seeing the missing entrepreneur back in their midst. The stranger and a freshly confident Will, only added a sense of puzzlement to the already psychic cocktail.

Grace's sparkling eyes moved slowly around the hushed gathering, fixed in a knowing gaze, before striding purposefully towards the recent participants in the shop floor confusion. What now? Suddenly and completely unexpectedly, the matriarch reached out her hand to each and every one of the stunned gathering, totally ignoring the reflexive stuttering, that attempted to issue from their dry mouths. Words, however, seemed meaningless in the reactivated chemistry that once more flowed between Self's founder and her beloved workforce. As if by magic, a harmonious cry rang out in unison, echoing its way around the shiny factory walls.

"Welcome back Ma'am. We're sorry we let you down. You know we're proud to work for you."

And so, the once great company was reborn; a restored enterprise in creative unity. Of course changes were made.

Grace granted the workforce an even greater role than before, each employee enjoying the freedom to walk into her office and share their innovative ideas for Self. Rukah and Will, unsurprisingly, hit it off as Grace's boundless charisma flowed through the pair to permeate the whole company. Competitors were amazed; Self Incorporated were well and truly back in business; back where they belonged.

42

Will I or Won't I? ~ Part 3

I hope that you enjoyed my little parable regarding *Will*. I'm sure that you have your own particular take on the interpretation of the tale. Truth tends to come in an appropriate guise when our hearts are thirsty for further Light. I believe all revelation to be intensely personal as it swirls around the darkened caverns of our Love starved psyches. However, with that in mind, may I share some thoughts that have been doing the rounds of my own unconscious regarding Self Incorporated.

Many of us believe our Will to be a unique gift, given to us by a separate and distinct divinity, or in common parlance, by a god. Such has been the traditional take on Will in the Western religious mindset of the past two millennia. This model of the Will tends to suggest that it requires continual realignment with Divine purpose, otherwise it easily slips off and does its own thing, often labelled selfishness. The result of such a dualistic mindset, is intense psychic pressure, an over-the-top vigilance that destroys our genuine sense of rest and self-esteem.

So here's what I've been pondering: rather than *having*

> *Because I/we have always been more than enough, always been Imago Dei, love, loved and loving!*
>
> Dylan Morrison

a Will are we not, in fact, the Divine Will *itself*? Our encounter with Spirit Breath hasn't dragged us *back* to the Divine Will but has *enlightened* us to the fact that we never possessed a separate Will in the first place. One's sense of an individual Will is, I suggest, an ego illusion, one projected onto the screen of our consciousness in order to maintain the myth of separation, the very fuel of much religious thought and practice. —YES—

Within faith communities, rebellion and its resulting separation are the necessary prerequisites to conversion and a return to Divine Union.

Once I was lost but now I'm found!

Yet, suppose the story of return and redemption are only etchings on the surface of an even deeper Reality viz. that we never really left Divine Will in the first place, for we can't leave Ourselves. Our dream-like state of separation, rebellion and redemption are, instead, virtual tutorials, serving the greater purpose of our deepening Awareness of Divine Love and our place within it. Such a shift in our thinking, especially if we've been programmed by a traditional religious model, can have a dynamic, life changing effect on our daily experience.

We are the Divine Will. We always have been, presently are, and always will be that Divine Delight, manifested within this holographic space-time world. Much of our internal suffering comes through resistance to the reality

Not that I/we are God but that we are in God and in Him we live, and move and have our Being! Acts 17:28

Way Beyond The Blue

presenting itself before us, to the psychic storms seemingly coming our way. Awakening to the nature of our virtual world, we can afford to *just go with the flow*. Such a release from ego control paradoxically creates a beneficial change in the *reality* facing us. In other words, the more we resist our programme, the more we suffer. The more we let go, the more Divine Love can realign our projected experience with Ultimate Reality. The storehouses of Divine Will are packed with an infinity of scripted possibilities.

As we awaken to find ourselves within Sacred Unity, may we enjoy our temporal birthright viz. to walk with Spirit Presence through this earthly *field of dreams*. Let's share the joy of being the Divine Will with all those still convinced of their inherent struggle for survival in this ego-driven world, called *life*.

living out of my/one's True Self

Epilogue

When I arrived in the historic, English, cathedral city of Lincoln back in 2009, I'd no idea what lay in front of me. Feeling like a prisoner, recently released from a cultural confinement, one that had defined me for all of my fifty four years, I wondered what would happen next. Much to my surprise my inner Voice immediately got on the ball, gently instructing me to write my life story thus far. And so, my first book, *The Prodigal Prophet*, was born; my spiritual memoirs of life in Northern Irish religion and its accompanying roller coaster events.

At the same time, I also sensed that I was to enter into the embryonic world of religious blogging. Why I wasn't sure, but today I think I know. Most bloggers of a spiritual nature seem to have life all sorted out, much like the fundamentalist Christian believers among whom I once counted myself. The web contained a real Vanity Fair of religious and spiritual products often for sale or freely received after a monetary donation. Was this world much different from the one I'd left all those decades before? I painfully concluded that, tragically, it was much the same.

So why was I being led to become Dylan Morrison the blogger? I suspected that I was to be a catalyst between different spiritual camps viz. the Christian camp and the Mind, Body, Spirit camp. Like a somewhat crazy, little, Irish bumble-bee, pollinating differing psycho-spiritual flowers along the Way, I was to visit all with an open heart, learning to receive before passing on my prophetic two cents worth of Truth. It would prove to be a tricky and often frustrating task. One long established tribe claimed a monopoly on Yeshua, or Jesus as they familiarly labelled him, whilst the other relatively esoteric clan had purposely ignored Him or patronisingly left Him in their spiritual pantheon, as one among many ascended masters. I could understand each tribe's position but not settle in either, believing Yeshua to have a unique Divine message for all mankind.

Frankly, most Christians seemed obsessed on St. Paul's take on Yeshua's crucifixion and claimed resurrection almost to the extent that if He'd only turned up on earth during Holy Week it wouldn't have really mattered. After all, from their eternal perspective, He was only on Earth to die and be raised. Most Christian teaching and programming is focused around these climactically interpreted events with Yeshua's take on daily spirituality left aside for the silent, and dare I say it, slightly weird minority.

My observations of the whole Mind, Body, Spirit scene suggested that many adherents had been raised and deeply wounded within traditional religious families and sects. Interestingly, but perhaps not surprisingly, many of these alternative seekers seemed to have escaped as quickly as possible from a strict Catholic upbringing. Their ditching of *the baby* Yeshua along with the accompanying *muddied*

Christian bathwater, was a sad but totally understandable stance for them to take on their road to healing and life purpose. In a defining twist, many fundamentalists of the New Age genre avoided Yeshua like the plague, unlike their Christian counterparts who never stopped talking about Him.

My hope is, that in some small measure, 'Way Beyond The Blue' will help those of us with our feet firmly planted in either of these opposing camps of *metaphysical meaning* to experience firsthand the shocking inclusivity of Yeshua, and that of His Love Divinity, *Abba*. May our distorted characterization of the *other tribe* melt away as together we stretch out our hands to embrace the essence of Spirit and, consequentially, all those on the Way Home.

Glossary of Important Terms

Listed below are definitions of a few key words used in the text.

Mimesis = the ability to copy or imitate someone outside the Self without prior conscious thought.

Mimesis is the subconscious imitative reflex with which we are equipped in order to learn from significant others, e.g. our parents' during infancy. All learning comes through copying. Indeed, we are wired to receive a unique Divine *desire frequency or Will* and conform to it. However, something primal has gone wrong in our inherited mimetic settings, resulting in us regularly absorbing the desires of others, possessing them and believing them to be our very own. This dysfunctional process initiates the process of human rivalry, one which usually results in some form of expulsion or violent act.

Skewed Desire = a horizontal or angled desire that latches onto the desire emanating from a fellow human being.

The desire transmitter is either someone on the same *level as ourselves,* e.g. a brother, sister, friend or, alternatively, an *authority figure or model,* someone we look up to e.g. a parent, teacher, boss, sporting celebrity, film star etc.

Scapegoat Mechanism = the human dynamic whereby individuals and communities release the build up of desire rivalry and its accompanying tensions.

In this process a victim or subgroup is randomly chosen, to carry the blame for the flaws appearing in the psycho-social life of an individual or, alternatively, within the greater community. Such a selection often targets a victim that somehow appears *different.* The scapegoating process usually involves a number of increasingly intense stages, e.g targeted humor, gossip, verbal and often physical violence before the *other* is finally frozen out or physically expelled from the community. This *sending away* may ultimately take the form of murder or community sanctioned killing. Once the victim has been removed a strange cathartic peace returns to permeate the community in question, thus reinforcing their belief that their social problems were indeed the *fault* of their designated victim.

Sacrificial Religion = A belief system whereby a victim, either animal or human is killed in order to placate an offended divinity.

A victim of the scapegoat mechanism may, inadvertently, take on the nature of a divinity following their communal demise. If their violent departure has brought about a much sought after peace, then they're either perceived as a god, a great dispenser of peace or as one to have successfully appeased the god whose righteous anger first led to the cracks appearing within our individual life or community. The victim may even become a *devil-god*, one who causes the problems but also fixes them through their death.

Culture = a way of thinking that has emerged to help human society cope with the violence and rivalry of skewed desire.

Culture comprises, rites/ritual, myths, laws, structures. All culture is a form of religion and all religion cultural.

Rites/Ritual =dramatic re-enactments of the original, violent expulsion of the victim

Myths = the story of the scapegoat and its expulsion as described by the scapegoating community. Of course, the scapegoat may have another version of past events.

Structures = Organizations and institutions that form hierarchies to let folk know their place or station within the community. e.g. family, government, courts, faith groups. The aim of these is to enforce laws, both spoken and unspoken by means of distancing us from our desire models. The greater the distance the more unlikely we are to absorb or steal the desire of another.

Queendom of God = Commonly referred to as the *Kingdom* of God within traditional Christian thought, this inner space is where we enter into mimesis with Divine Love, having disengaged from the dysfunctional effects of skewed mimesis, viz absorbing and rivaling the desire of others.

About The Author

Dylan Morrison is a spiritual author, poet and Yeshua thinker, presently living in the historic, cathedral city of Lincoln, England.

Raised in Northern Ireland, Dylan has a great empathy with all who've travelled through dysfunctional religious movements in their search for meaning. He writes to expose religious control whilst bringing hope to those who've suffered from various forms of spiritual abuse.

Morrison believes that the mysticism of Yeshua bar Yosef, the Nazarene prophet-teacher, holds the key for those searching for an authentic spirituality; one that satisfies the hunger of angst-ridden, 21st century man.

Also By Dylan Morrison

The Prodigal Prophet

A roller coaster tale of religious disillusionment and Divine hijacking.

&

Bolts From The Blue

An out of the box inspirational reader

Available in paperback, Kindle and other ebook formats

CPSIA information can be obtained
at www.ICGtesting.com
Printed in the USA
LVHW020017241218
601557LV00017B/505/P